CURRENT REGIONAL ISSUES

*Illinois, Indiana, Michigan,
Minnesota, Ohio, Wisconsin*

John P. Blair
Wright State University

Wayne D. Carroll
University of Wisconsin–Eau Claire

Richard W. Lichty
University of Minnesota–Duluth

The Dryden Press
Harcourt Brace College Publishers

Fort Worth Philadelphia San Diego New York
Orlando Austin San Antonio Toronto Montreal
London Sydney Tokyo

Requests for permission to make copies of any part of the work should be mailed to: Permissions Department, Harcourt Brace College Publishers, 6277 Sea Harbor Drive, Orlando, FL 32887-6777.

Address for Editorial Correspondence
The Dryden Press, 301 Commerce Street, Suite 3700, Fort Worth, TX 76102

Address for Orders
The Dryden Press, 6277 Sea Harbor Drive, Orlando, FL 32887
1-800-782-4479, or 1-800-433-0001 (in Florida)

ISBN: 0-03-002052-2

Printed in the United States of America

3 4 5 6 7 8 9 0 1 2   066   9 8 7 6 5 4 3 2 1

The Dryden Press
Harcourt Brace College Publishers

CONTENTS

PREFACE

Students of economics face the challenge of understanding how economic concepts tie in with problems and issues in the real world around them. *Current Regional Issues* attempts to provide economic insight into problems and issues confronting a specific U.S. region. The supplements establish links between concepts taught at the principles level and regional issues students are aware of through newspapers or television.

Each of the ten supplements is a collection of brief essays written by Principles of Economics instructors at schools in the specific region and covers topics students in that area should find interesting.

ABOUT THE AUTHORS

John P. Blair is currently the Belinda A. Bruns Professor of Economics at Wright State University in Dayton, Ohio. He received his PhD in Economics from West Virginia University. His fields of interest include economic development and regional economics. Professor Blair has published widely in journals such as *Urban Affairs Quarterly, Review of Regional Studies,* and *Economic Development Quarterly.* His latest book is *Urban and Regional Economics* (Irwin, 1991). Professor Blair has served as a consultant to businesses and governments and is a member of the Montgomery Planning Commission.

Wayne Carroll is currently teaching in the Department of Economics at the University of Wisconsin–Eau Claire. He received his PhD in Economics from the University of Minnesota, and his undergraduate degree from the University of Chicago. His research interests include microeconomic theory, applied microeconomics, and industrial organization, with a special emphasis on applications of microeconomic theory to environmental economics. Professor Carroll is also interested in growth patterns and business fluctuations in the regional economy.

Richard Lichty is currently Head of the Department of Economics at the University of Minnesota–Duluth. He has taught economics at the undergraduate level for over twenty-three years and has won national and university awards for excellence and innovations in teaching. Professor Lichty's fields of interests are regional and urban economics. He has published several articles in professional journals and currently serves as a member of the editorial board of *Regional Science Perspectives*. Professor Lichty has also served as Director of the University of Minnesota's Center for Economic Education.

THE CENTRAL CITY: SUBURBAN INCOME GAP AND URBAN POVERTY

John P. Blair

Wright State University

The central cities of the major metroplitan areas in the Great Lakes region have higher poverty rates than their more affluent suburban neighbors. While this problem is prominent in the Great Lakes states, it exists in almost all large urban areas in the United States. The poverty of many central city residents in comparison with neighboring jurisdictions is interconnected with a variety of issues including racial and income segregation, fiscal problems, and social pathologies. Furthermore, some "vicious circles" can hinder solutions or lead to a worsening of the economic problem.

Before examining central city poverty in detail, it is useful to distinguish between various parts of urban regions. "Entire metropolitan area" is defined by the U.S. Census Bureau as a group of counties with a large population nucleus (a city or "twin cities" such as Minneapolis–St. Paul) together with adjacent counties that have a high degree of social and economic integration. The nucleus is referred to as the central city. The area with the heaviest concentration of economic activity within the central city is the central business district (CBD). While the central business districts usually appear prosperous, they are normally surrounded by low income areas and often isolated from the rest of the metropolitan economy. The suburbs constitute the metropolitan

Table 1 ✦ Central City-Suburban Income Comparisons

City	Income Ratio 1987	Median Household Central City	Income Change Suburbs
Cleveland	42.8	–13.9	–3.7
Chicago	45.0	2.0	1.1
Detroit	48.9	–20.5	–2.4
Milwaukee	50.2	–12.6	0.4
Dayton	56.2	–3.6	–.8
Indianapolis	57.5	2.9	–0.4
Columbus	59.2	6.6	3.1
Cincinnati	66.4	–1.7	–0.1
Pittsburgh	67.0	–8.2	–10.8
Minneapolis	70.1	1.9	3.6

area beyond the central city. Suburbs include other large cities, such as Wakeagen near Chicago, as well as small towns and unincorporated areas. Farms even fall within metropolitan areas.

The income of central city residents contrasts sharply with suburban residents. Table 1 shows the income ratio of central city residents to suburban residents for major metropolitan areas in the Great Lakes states. The lower the ratio, the greater the intrametropolitan income disparity. Nationwide among large metropolitan areas, the average central city–suburban income ratio is about 60 percent. Seven of the ten Great Lakes states have greater disparities (lower city–suburban income ratios) than the average. Cleveland, Chicago, and Detroit all have ratios indicating that central city residents earn less than half the income of suburban residents. The city–suburb income ratios may actually understate the extent of geographic disparity because inner city neighborhoods generally have much lower incomes than the rest of the central city.

Some observers might suggest that the metropolitan income gaps are acceptable because poor people can be expected to live together in neighborhoods with deteriorating housing and few amenities. After all, the poor have less of almost everything. While this perspective may have some merit, it overlooks the fact that as central city economies deteriorate, solutions that could reverse the decline become more difficult to implement.

The isolation of low income individuals and families in inner city neighborhoods sets the stage for a vicious circle of cumulative decline. Young children may lack adequate role models of mainstream economic success. Illegal activities and welfare may seem like normal and reasonable alternatives to conventional life pursuits. Such attitudes may contribute to the development of a permanent underclass. Furthermore many middle- and upper-income families move to the suburbs to escape externalities such as crime and congestion associated with living near low-income neighborhoods. The process of cumulative decline may also operate through governmental fiscal systems. Large concentrations of low-income families create heavy financial burdens on city governments. The poor are a costly population to serve because of their many needs—more social services and police protection for example. Detroit and Cleveland have experienced such severe fiscal problems. At the same time, it is difficult to raise tax revenue from the poor. As a result many city governments have had to raise taxes on middle-income residents in order to pay for services. Middle-income residents have, in turn, moved to the suburbs to obtain a more satisfactory mix of taxes and services. As middle-income citizens have left the central city, the income disparity has increased, economic opportunities for inner city residents have been lost, and fiscal pressures on cities have mounted.

Great Lakes cities have developed a number of policies designed to address the problem of low central city incomes. One solution has been to attempt to attract jobs to poor neighborhoods through enterprise zone programs. An enterprise zone is a geographic area usually zoned for industrial activities. Frequently such areas are vacant industrial properties. Businesses that locate in enterprise zones normally receive tax breaks and other special assistance from the city and state governments. For instance, a firm locating in an enterprise zone may be entitled to a reduced property tax rate, special low-interest loans, and assistance in training workers. The extent of public assistance often depends upon the willingness of the business to hire low-income city residents.

Most enterprise zones in the Great Lakes states can be considered successful in the sense that businesses have located to the designated areas. However, many of the better paying jobs have gone to suburban residents. Furthermore, the greater the poverty and related social problems in the inner city, the more difficult it is to attract new businesses and the less employable local residents tend to be. To the extent that inner city residents are unable to obtain new jobs because of low levels of education or employment skills, the benefits from the enterprise zone projects obviously drop.

Central city governments have also focused efforts on central business district revitalization. For instance Cincinnati's CBD plans call for attracting middle-income residents downtown, strengthening retail business, and expanding convention center and entertainment facilities. Most downtown development plans for other cities have similar goals. However, downtown revitalization efforts have been constrained by the fact that historic problems in or near the central cities have decreased resources and created an unattractive image.

Often downtown investments fail to alleviate the poverty problems in the inner city. For instance, Detroit's revitalization efforts have been criticized because they resulted in a large complex of office towers, called Renaissance Center, that was deliberately isolated from nearby inner city neighborhoods. The isolation was intended to shield Renaissance Center from inner city problems, but it also prevented inner city residents from receiving as many benefits from the revitalization as they otherwise would have. Another shortcoming between downtown revitalization and living improvement for inner city residents is a serious mismatch between the types of job openings in the central city and the skills inner city residents have. Job growth in central business districts has been fastest in jobs requiring high school and college educations. In fact, the income generated by jobs located in the central city actually pay more than suburban jobs. Again, the well paying downtown jobs tend to be held by suburban residents. Thus, the low income of inner city residents can be attributed at least in part to an inability to get jobs in the nearby CBD.

While the educational requirements for central city jobs have been increasing, performance in central city schools has decreased. Typical of such schools, the performance of central city school districts in Ohio are shown in Table 2. Each of the central city school districts scored well below the state average.

The poor performance of central city schools illustrates another of the vicious circles that affect inner city economic performance. Social and economic problems of students and their families have contributed to poor performance, which in turn resulted in unemployment and other social and economic problems.

In order to break the cycle of poor academic performance and socioeconomic problems, the Dayton public schools developed a multi-million dollar program to team social workers with teachers and "at risk" students— students with social problems likely to result in poor performance. The social workers visited student homes and helped families obtain public resources that could enhance the home environment. Unfortunately, after several years, improvement in the academic performance of students in this program were small. The program was abandoned.

Table 2 ✦ Rankings and Composite Test Score Index: 1990

City	Score	Rank*
Cleveland	43.89	597
Columbus	49.11	478
Cincinnati	46.00	564
Toledo	48.56	499
Akron	47.11	543
Dayton	44.22	586
Youngstown	47.22	535
Ohio Average	53.53	305

*Out of 610 districts

Training for adults is also an important part of efforts to improve incomes of inner city residents. Most Great Lakes areas have training programs that tend to be either skill development and/or behavioral training designed to affect worker attitudes toward jobs, provide job search skills, and teach appropriate work behavior. Unfortunately, the benefits of job training are frustrated when jobs are not increasing.

Another solution to inner city poverty is relocation. The theory is that if inner city families had access to jobs in the faster growing suburbs, they would have a better chance of attaining employment. While suburban jobs do not pay as much as the prestigious central business district jobs, they are better matched with the existing skills of inner city residents.

The Gautreaux Project in Chicago has demonstrated that relocation to suburban areas may help some inner city residents in terms of both employment opportunities and education. The Gautreaux Project began when the federal courts found the Chicago Housing Authority guilty of racial discrimination. The housing authority was placing blacks in housing projects in predominantly black areas, thus contributing to the metropolitan wide problem of racial segregation.

Part of the remedy was to require the Chicago Housing authority to relocate many African-Americans from the predominantly black housing projects into predominantly white areas in the city of Chicago and in the suburbs. One-third of the families in the projects moved to within the city of Chicago and two-thirds moved into housing in Chicago's suburbs.

A comparison of those who moved to the city with those who moved to the suburbs is interesting. Before the move both the "city movers" and the "suburb movers" had similar demographic profiles. Typically, the families were African-American female-headed households receiving welfare, unemployed, with two or three children. After the move, 51 percent of the city-mover household heads had jobs compared to 64 percent of the suburb movers. Of the city-mover children, 80 percent graduated from high school compared with 95 percent of suburb movers. Eighty percent of the suburb movers continued their education beyond high school (27 percent in four year colleges) compared to 21 percent for city movers (4 percent in four year colleges). Youth work patterns were similar. Forty-one percent of city movers and 75 percent of suburb movers youths were working. In terms of income, 21 percent of suburban movers and 5 percent of city movers were earning over $6.50 per hour. While comparable data on families who remained in segregated inner city public housing was not collected, the performance of both city and suburb movers far exceeded the performance of typical public housing occupants. Unfortunately, relocation and housing assistance is an expensive solution and many neighborhoods resist programs to decentralize public housing.

An intriguing strategy for enhancing economic prospects of inner city residents is building greater cooperation between the central city and its suburban neighbors. Recent evidence has shown that central city and suburban economic growth go hand in hand. When average central city income increases, so does suburban income. However Table 1 indicates that the correlation is not strong. Nevertheless, many observers believe that central cities and suburbs share common economic futures because they complement each other. The findings suggest that cities and suburbs should cooperate in economic development efforts.

Indianapolis is an example of an area that has experienced a great deal of success. The success has been attributed in large part to "unigov," a plan initiated in the early 1970s that consolidated taxes, planning, and public services. Because of unigov, the city was able to effectively pursue an economic development strategy based on attracting sports events. It is unlikely that the cluster of downtown sports facilities would have been built without the cooperation of the suburbs brought about by unigov.

Solutions to the problem of inner city poverty involving city–suburb cooperation are subject to another vicious circle. As central city problems increase, suburbs become increasingly reluctant to establish strong partnerships with the central city. Simultaneously, central cities will have fewer resources to contribute and more problems requiring help.

No single solution is likely to eliminate the central city–suburb income gap because the problem of inner city poverty is so complex. The greater the central city–suburb income gap and the greater the extent of inner city poverty, the more difficult it is to implement solutions.

REFERENCES

Ledebur, Larry C. and William R. Barnes. *Metropolitan Disparities and Economic Growth.* Washington, D.C., The National League of Cities, March, 1992.

Rush, David. *Cities Without Suburbs.* Washington, D.C. The Woodrow Wilson Center Press, 1993.

LOCAL EFFORTS TO ATTRACT BUSINESS

John Blair
Wright State University

Noel McKinney
Wright State University

The slow employment and income growth of the Great Lakes Region, coupled with reductions in federal economic development programs, have placed a burden on state and local governments to encourage economic development within their region. Most Great Lakes states provide the following types of subsidies: 1) tax abatements; 2) infrastructure improvements; 3) job training; 4) grants for construction and other purposes; 5) start-up and expansion loans; 6) bond issues that companies repay at low interest rates. Table 1 on page 10 shows state governmental economic development appropriations. In addition to state spending, city governments and other agencies are working to create jobs at the local level. The increased role of states and localities has created controversy regarding the proper role of local governments in economic development.

There are two broad philosophic approaches regarding the proper role of local governments in economic development. Those individuals who follow the laissez faire tradition regarding economic policy see little role for government beyond efficiently carrying out traditional government functions. They argue that the invisible hand could alleviate economic development problems without government initiatives. For instance, if a state or locality is experienc-

Table 1 ✦ State Appropriations for Economic Development: 1988

State	Per Capita Appropriation	Total Appropriations
Indiana	$10.03	$ 8,550,500
Michigan	63.38	30,702,200
Minnesota	5.53	22,895,000
Ohio	7.64	82,104,651
Wisconsin	3.51	16,772,100
Pennsylvania	20.77	246,240,000

Source: National Association of State Development Agencies, 1988 State Economic Development Survey.

ing high unemployment and commercial property vacancies, then according to the laissez faire tradition, wages and other costs of production will fall. The declines in the cost of business will attract new enterprises, contributing to local job and wealth creation. At the same time, unemployed workers will leave the area, thus reducing the local unemployment rate.

The laissez faire approach has generally been rejected by local policy makers for several reasons. First, some of the assumptions necessary for a well functioning market are absent in reality. For instance, the laissez faire model includes the assumption that production costs will fall and alleviate unemployment. In reality, wages and prices tend to be inflexible, particularly in a downward direction. The high rate of unionization in the Great Lakes region contributes to wage rigidities. In addition, many employers pay above-market wages simply to encourage workers to work harder. Consequently, business costs may not decline and new businesses may not be attracted to the area.

Second, the laissez faire model also assumes perfect information. However, economic development in large Great Lakes areas is hampered by inaccurate information about local problems. Dayton and Toledo are often perceived as having destructive labor–management problems, although the problems do not appear to be that significant by those who know the region well. Nevertheless, the poor image probably discourages economic development.

Third, resources are not as mobile as is implied by the model. Unemployed workers may be tied to their local areas in numerous ways (family ties, social relationships, difficulty in selling a home, and so forth). These costs may prevent the unemployed from relocating to job growth areas.

Finally, even if the markets would respond as described in the laissez faire model, it may take years before the problem is reduced. Thus anxious politicians may be unwilling to wait for the laissez faire approach solve their problems, to bring about a solution. This time concern reflects Keynes's attitude towards long adjustment periods in the classical model when he said, "In the long run, we are all dead."

On the other side of the argument lies the interventionist approach where government officials directly encourage businesses to locate operations in their communities, generally by offering firms a variety of direct and indirect subsidies. Unfortunately, these enticements often lead to inefficient competition between Great Lakes states in a zero sum game that results in firms locating where they receive the largest benefits while not creating net new jobs for the region as a whole.

The location decision of the Navistar Corporation is an example of intergovernmental competition that resulted in taxpayer costs but no net benefit to the Great Lakes region as a whole. In the mid-1980s Navistar (then called International Harvester), headquartered in Chicago, Illinois, announced that as part of a consolidation plan it would close one of two Great Lakes region plants, either a plant located in Fort Wayne, Indiana, or Springfield, Ohio. The two communities were thus thrown into competition.

Both communities worked with their state governments to create incentive packages. After Navistar considered the offers, the facility in Indiana was closed and the one in Ohio remained open. In discussing the decision, Navistar officials commented that the incentive packages proposed by Indiana and Ohio were about equal. They selected the Ohio site because the existing plant was more modern and hence more efficient. In other words, the subsidy offers cancelled each other out. If neither state had offered an incentive package, the Ohio site probably would have been kept open anyway and taxpayers could have saved the cost of the subsidy given to Navistar.

The problems with the way some local economic development programs have been implemented have led policy makers to reevaluate the principles behind economic development programs. One approach centers on correcting market failures. By considering policies designed to correct market failure, the interventionist and laissez faire traditions may be bridged. Advocates of laissez faire concede that market failures do occur and may require government intervention.

Consider the existence of externalities that have been used to justify government provision of many goods and services. Private markets might fail to raise sufficient funds to support economic development. A firm's decision to

Table 2 ✦ Hypothetical Benefits from a Business Start-Up

	Potential benefits without incentives	Potential distribution after incentives
Benefit to firm	*$–10*	*$1*
Benefits to community	*$30*	*$19*

locate operations in a particular community could benefit a wide variety of individuals. Even those individuals who failed to contribute to economic development programs may benefit. The location of a new polymer facility in Akron, Ohio, is an example of an action that may contribute to the overall strength of the region as a center for polymer production and thus help existing producers and suppliers. The new firm or expanded firm may also help taxpayers if its tax payment exceeds increased public service costs. It may provide benefits for other retail businesses as workers spend their income locally, creating a local multiplier effect. Perhaps the most important externalities are the benefits received by workers who get jobs that pay above their reservation wage.

Because of the high costs of organizing all of the potential beneficiaries and because of the potential that many beneficiaries will attempt to free ride, the private market may be unable to provide necessary incentives to capture the externalities. Accordingly, local governments have felt justified in acting for individual citizens.

Table 2 places the situation into a theoretical model and illustrates how locational subsidies may result in greater efficiency. Suppose a firm is considering locating in Charleston, Illinois. No other location is feasible. If the firm were to start operations it would generate $30 of external benefits to residents annually. However, the –$10 profit indicates that the firm could not operate profitably without a government subsidy. Thus the firm would not start operating.

Suppose, however, that the government taxed citizens $11 and used the money to finance incentives designed to attract the firm. The firm could then operate profitably. The $1 annual profit the firm would receive after the subsidy represents above normal profits. However, citizens will have to pay $11 in extra taxes resulting in net benefits of $19, not $30. Nevertheless, by offering economic development incentives, citizens as a group benefited.

Of course the fact that benefits for citizens *could* be gained does not imply that governments *will always* act in the best interest of citizens. If an incentive package of over $30 had been offered in the example, community residents would have been worse off due to the excessive subsidy. The government would have given the firm more in subsidies than the community received in benefits. Many critics believe this situation is common.

The case of the General Motors Pole Town plant is an example that may represent a locality over-subsiding a facility for political reasons. When GM, the largest employer in Detroit, announced that it was considering relocating a plant, the community, and the plant employees in particular were naturally concerned. They looked to the local government to intervene. Detroit offered GM a subsidy package of $200,000,000 to remain in the area. Many observers contended that the subsidy package was excessive. The desire of politicians to please their constituents coupled with their lack of knowledge about competing deals resulted in the excessive "giveaway." Because the costs of a business location subsidy are generally paid in the politically distant future, an elected official may have an incentive to overpay for a major business location to help his or her election next year.

Imperfect information is another market failure that can be corrected by local government economic development efforts. If businesses lack the information needed to make wise decisions, they may not consider Great Lakes locations, even though they may be satisfactory. Cleveland, Ohio has had a particularly bad reputation. Consequently, economic development officials in Cleveland have been focusing efforts on image building, including advertising in magazines targeting businesses that may be interested in locating to Cleveland. Pittsburgh, Pennsylvania, exemplifies a city that had a successful image building campaign.

Capital markets represent another area where imperfect information may limit economic development. Officials in many Great Lakes cities believe that investors overlook good investments in their areas or believe the risks are higher than they really are. Consequently many states are undertaking efforts to encourage investments. The Primus fund in Cleveland, Ohio, is a $30,000,000 limited partnership backed in part by public capital that is constrained to investments in Ohio. Ohio and Michigan have made direct investments in new enterprises with state money. If the businesses are successful, the states will receive returns consistent with the equity risks they are taking.

The closure of GM's Willow Run assembly plant in Lansing, Michigan, presents an interesting twist on policies of subsidizing business locations. As part of its consolidation plan, GM moved to close the facility employing 2,500 workers and moved the production to Texas.

The Willow Run plant is an old facility; in fact it was in use during

World War II to produce bombers. As part of a modernization effort in 1984 and 1988, the local government granted GM tax abatements in order to induce the plant to stay in Lansing.

When GM announced it was closing the Lansing facility, local officials sued. They claimed that when they agreed to tax breaks in order to induce GM to stay, they had entered an implicit contract. GM had agreed to stay in lansing and Lansing had agreed to give GM the tax abatement. GM argued that keeping Willow Run open would cost the company $300 million per year and disrupt its plans to cut costs.

How would you decide the case? In a lower court the judge ruled in favor of Lansing and ordered that the plant remain open. However, the case was overturned by the Michigan Supreme Court, so GM is continuing with its plan to close the facility. The Supreme Court, however, did suggest that GM might have to repay the value of the tax abatements it received in the past.

Do development incentives actually help create jobs in local areas? Economic development practitioners generally believe that incentive programs are necessary to compete with other areas. However academic literature has provided no conclusive generalizations.

REFERENCES   .

Bartik, Timothy J., "The Market Failure Approach to Regional Economic Development Policy," *Economic Development Quarterly,* Vol. 4, No. 4, November 1990, pp. 361-370.

Blair, John P., Rudy Fichtenbaum, and James Swaney, "The Market for Jobs: Locational Decisions and the Competition for Economic Development," *Urban Affairs Quarterly,* Vol. 10, No. 1, 1984, pp. 64-76.

IMPACT OF JAPANESE INVESTMENT IN THE GREAT LAKES REGION

John P. Blair
Wright State University

Carole R. Endres
Wright State University

Concerns have been raised about recent foreign investment in the United States. While there has always been substantial foreign investment, the criticisms have arisen at a time when Japanese investors have become prominent. Critics contend that foreign ownership undermines the ability of the United States to control its political and economic future. Foreign ownership may bring with it greater foreign political influence and also shift the site of important economic decisions affecting Americans to foreign countries.

Other analysts point out that foreign investment benefits U.S. residents principally by generating employment and tax revenues. Furthermore, U.S. investors seek overseas investments, so why should not foreign investors invest in the United States?

Excluding California, which has the highest number of start-ups, the Great Lakes region accounted for the bulk of Japanese locations. The increased Japanese investment came at a time of declining automobile production by the "Big Three" auto-makers and declines in manufacturing in general. Because of the need to create new manufacturing jobs, states have competed aggressively with one another for Japanese investments by offering direct financing of facilities, low interest loans, infrastructure improvements and tax abatements.

In 1985 Diamond-Star Motors (a joint venture between Mitsubishi Motors and Chrysler Corporation) announced that it would assemble automobiles in Bloomington–Normal, Illinois. Plans called for construction of a two million square foot plant on over 630 acres of undeveloped land. When in full operation the facility was expected to produce 240,000 small cars annually and employ 2,500–2,900 people. The story of how Illinois was able to attract the facility is a story of cooperation among local governments within a framework of interstate competition.

Illinois attracted the Diamond-Star facility in a heated contest with Indiana and Michigan. The Illinois Department of Commerce and Community Affairs extended $88.2 million in incentives to Diamond-Star in the form of training, site acquisition, and construction of pubic infrastructure.

Most analysts believe that the economic development incentives offered by Indiana and Michigan were comparable to Illinois' subsidy offer. (This belief is difficult to confirm because negotiations between Diamond-Star and each of the states were confidential. Only after deals are structured are details made public.) What tipped the balance towards Bloomington–Normal, Illinois?

One possibility is that Illinois officials presented an incentive package that already contained an agreement between local units of government. Illinois took the initiative in bringing local governments into a unified bargaining unit. Therefore they saved Diamond-Star executives the necessity of negotiating local as well as state agreements. Thus, Diamond-Star officials may have felt assured of future cooperation between the state and local governments. Furthermore, Mitsubishi reportedly favored the Bloomington–Normal site because it is close to Chicago, Illinois State University, and the super conducting research facilities at the University of Illinois in Champaign–Urbana.

Income and employment benefits of the Diamond-Star facility have been divided into impacts during the construction phase and during the operations phase. Nearly 500 people were employed during the construction phase and another 149 were estimated to be employed indirectly in supplying the construction industry and through induced consumer spending. Thus an employment multiplier of 1.3 (649/500) is implied. In the operations phase, direct employment has been estimated to be slightly less than 3,000 employees but after the multiplier effects are registered, employment is forecast to be about 6,800. Not surprisingly, the largest sector impact is in durable goods. While the impacts are significant, they could have been even greater except for the fact that 40 to 60 percent of inputs used by Diamond-Star were to be imported from Japan.

The model also estimated the distribution of impacts throughout the state. Not surprisingly, the Bloomington–Normal area experienced the greatest number of benefits. However, major impacts were also projected for the Chicago area because the manufacturers there may be major suppliers.

Honda of America is the fourth largest automobile producer in the United States. It is the brightest star in a constellation of Japanese automobile-related facilities in south-central Ohio. The story of Honda in south-central Ohio is the development of an automobile-related complex over many years and was the outgrowth of many sequential decisions. In 1977 Honda invested $35 million in a motorcycle plant. By 1988, the investment had grown to over $1.2 billion and included major automobile facilities.

Several primary factors led to the decision to produce the Accord in south-central Ohio. First, Ohio and Honda began a solid relationship as early as 1977 when the company started producing motorcycles. The negotiations that resulted in the motorcycle facility established a working relationship between Honda and state officials.

Second, threats of government restrictions on Japanese automobile imports helped convince Honda officials that they needed a U.S. production site. Honda motorcycles benefitted greatly when President Reagan limited motorcycle imports in order to assist Harley-Davidson, a U.S. corporation. During the 1980s there were numerous political calls for Japanese automobile quotas and the Japanese were forced to "voluntarily" limit automobile imports.

Third, south-central Ohio also was a good location because it is close to Columbus (the state capital), urban amenities, interstate highways 75 and 70, other automobile suppliers, and the heart of the U.S. market. Finally, Honda received an attractive incentive package that included over $1 billion in various types of assistance over two decades.

The region received substantial benefits due to Honda's investments. The first automobile plant expansion added nearly 4,000 jobs to the economy. Honda initially limited recruiting efforts to residents within a 30 mile radius of its plant so most of the job benefits accrued to local residents. The jobs were particularly appreciated because there were cut-backs in other local facilities such as Goodyear and Nestlé. Honda operations propelled average income in the area. During the mid-1980s incomes increased well above the national average.

There are two important intangible benefits from the Honda automobile complex. First, residents have increased their awareness of international economic realities. For example, the local Chamber of Commerce markets the region to other international concerns as part of their growth strategies. Second, American producers and laborers have benefited from Japanese management practices. Having Honda in the area helped disseminate these ideas.

Perhaps the key to Honda's labor-management approach is the Associate System. The former President of Honda Manufacturing of America used the term "togetherness" to describe the Associate System.

There are five important elements to the associate system. First, while Honda America does not offer lifetime employment, compared to U.S. companies it is less likely to use lay-offs as an economic measure. Thereby, Honda management creates an atmosphere that suggests long-term commitment, and associates feel more secure about their employment. Second, when hiring, Honda seeks employees who are flexible, cooperative, and have a strong work ethic. The hiring process centers around the interview where managers and production associates jointly select new employees. This recruitment is more likely to select "team players."

Next, unlike large, bureaucratic U.S. companies, Honda has no job descriptions. Employees at all levels are expected to be output-oriented and work as part of a team. Managers and engineers are frequently seen on the shop floor discussing issues with line workers. Fourth, Honda has a commitment to job training as evidenced by the construction of a $3 million training center. In addition to technical training, some academic subjects including Japanese language and culture are available.

Finally, Honda's compensation package is roughly comparable to that of other U.S. auto companies. However, the hourly wage is supplemented by a bonus. Furthermore, the gap between top executives and shop floor workers is much less at Honda. The smaller spread probably helps reduce resentment and barriers to labor-management cooperation.

Many U.S. corporations have attempted to incorporate some of these Japanese management practices. The presence of a nearby, successful example of such practices has probably stimulated area producers to improve their labor management practices.

Mazda's decision to build its first U.S. automobile assembly plant in Flat Rock, Michigan, illustrates how a state attempted to attract a Japanese facility within the context of an overall economic development strategy. However, the pressure to attract the facility coupled with competition from other locations resulted in pressures to offer subsidies that appear inconsistent with that strategy.

In 1981 Ford Motor Company closed its casting center in Flat Rock, Michigan. The closing drastically reduced employment and the tax base for the area. Due to the Ford shut-down and other plant lay-offs, the area's unemployment rate reached nearly 16 percent in the early 1980s. Given the distressed nature of the community, it is not surprising that local officials were interested in the possibility of Mazda locating at the site of the former Ford facility.

Michigan's economic development strategy was based upon a desire to develop high-skilled, well-paying jobs. Officials realized that the state's past economic success was due to products and processing innovations. The state therefore designed a development path based on innovation requiring a good educational environment and a productive workforce. In effect the state rejected a strategy of wage cuts and massive tax giveaways (termed a "get-poor" strategy) as a development path in favor of a strategy that would attract facilities with high-wage work ("get smart"). This decision was prompted by the presence of a cluster of manufacturing facilities, a well-paid, manufacturing-oriented workforce, and an existing infrastructure including universities with strong industrial technology programs. Michigan's plan was to recapture its place as a leader in complex manufacturing. In terms of economic development efforts the strategy called for emphasizing manpower training, infrastructure improvement, and other measures to improve the productive assets of the region. The development approach eschews wage cuts and tax concessions.

Mazda's decision to open an advanced assembly plant, called the "factory of the future" was a perfect fit with the state's development strategy. It had both economic and symbolic importance. However, in developing an incentive package Michigan was aware that several other states were courting Mazda, most prominently Nebraska and North Carolina.

Michigan used a benefit-cost model to ensure that it did not give more in subsidies to Mazda than the state received in benefits. The incentive package offered to Mazda included: 1) a training program for Mazda employees (which included sending 300 supervisory employees to Japan); 2) low interest loans to help Mazda convert the Ford plant to a "factory of the future"; 3) improvements to roads, rail access, sewer, and water; and 4) a 100 percent tax abatement was given by local governments.

The locational incentives offered Mazda were generally consistent with

Table 1 ✦ Estimated Costs and Outcomes of Three Locational Decisions

Company	Location	Company Investment	State Investment	Direct Jobs Created	State Costs Per Job
Mitsubishi/ Chrysler (Diamond-Star)	Bloomington– Normal, IL	$500-700 million	$83.3 million	2,900	$28,724.14
Honda Complex	West Central Ohio	1.2 billion (over 10 years)	58.1 million (over 10 years)	5,840	9,948.00
Mazda	Flat Rock, Michigan	745-750 million	48.5 million	3,500	13,857.00

Source: H. Brinton Nelward and Heidi Hosbach Newman, "State Incentive Packages and the Industrial Location Decision," and John P. Blair, Carole Endres, and Rudy Fichtenbaum, "Japanese Automobile Investment in West-Central Ohio: Economic Development and Labor Management Issues" in Ernest J. Yanarella and William G. Green, *The Politics of Industrial Recruitment* (New York, Greenwood Press) 1990.

Michigan's "get smart" economic development strategy except for the tax abatement. The abatement, however, was considered necessary to attract Mazda. Essentially the importance of the "factory of the future" coupled with competition from other states made cost concessions necessary.

The granting of the local property tax abatements created some friction among local governments. Flat Rock, which bore the abatement costs, wanted Mazda to hire unemployed Flat Rock residents. However, Mazda and state officials had agreed to give hiring priorities to laid-off Ford employees in exchange for auto workers' flexibility regarding work rules. Fortunately, a compromise was worked out that gave local residents priority for non-union jobs.

The economic impact of Mazda's location was estimated using a benefit–cost model. The model projected that when the plant was in full production it would have 2,500 assembly jobs and produce 240,000 units annually. In estimating the overall impact of income and employment the model used a multiplier of 4.88, which appears to be excessively high.

Table 1 shows estimates of costs and direct jobs anticipated for the three Japanese facilities discussed above. It is clear that Illinois "paid" more per job than either Michigan or Ohio. However, Table 1 is not a complete analysis of the benefits and costs. The Ohio auto complex developed over many years so comparability is difficult. Furthermore, multiplier effects are ignored as are other benefits such as larger state tax collections. Also, many costs have been ignored such as local government contributions, greater congestion, and pollution. Nevertheless, the tone of the studies of Japanese plant location decisions suggests that the benefits far out-weighed the costs.

REFERENCES

Bachelor, Lynn W., "Michigan, Mazda, and the Factory of the Future: Evaluating Economic Development Initiatives" in *Economic Development Quarterly,* Vol. 5, No. 2, May 1991, pp. 114-125.

Cambell, Jr., Hanison S., "State and Regional Economic Impact of Diamond-Star Motors" in *Economic Development Review,* Vol. 7, No. 3, Summer 1989, pp. 31-34.

WELFARE REFORM IN WISCONSIN

Wayne Carroll

University of Wisconsin-Eau Claire

There is no debate about the need for programs to assist the poor and distressed in society. The states of Wisconsin, Minnesota, and Michigan have traditionally been unusually generous in their support for such efforts. But there are traps here: if the government assists the poor, they may become dependent on that help. The very nature of the welfare system might give fathers an incentive to leave their families.

In recent years the state of Wisconsin has tested some innovative welfare programs that aim to release welfare recipients from these traps. Some of these innovations—dubbed "workfare," "learnfare," and "bridefare" — have been highly controversial, because they place limits on the assistance that recipients can get. Wisconsin also has led the nation in efforts to collect child support payments from fathers who have left their children. These programs have served as models for welfare reform in other states and at the federal level. For example, Michigan's governor has proposed similar public assistance reforms or cuts in recent years.

The welfare traps are rooted in basic economics. Many people, whether poor or rich, will respond to a continuing cash grant by choosing not to work or, if they do work, to work fewer hours per week. In addition, the structure of welfare payments itself creates disincentives to work. Payments are made to those whose incomes are low and not those whose incomes are higher, so it must be the case that payments diminish as income rises. But this means that if a welfare recipient works harder to earn more income, some welfare payments might be lost. Economists refer to this as an implicit tax on the recipient's earnings.

If welfare benefits drop off quickly as the recipient's labor income rises, then the implicit tax rate is high, and this discourages work. But if the implicit tax rate is kept low by allowing recipients to keep a large share of their earnings, the level of income at which the welfare benefits finally run out is higher, and this tends to draw more people into the program. If welfare payments are eliminated completely when a particular income level is reached, a recipient might actually suffer a sharp drop in income if he or she earns a few more dollars and thus passes the cutoff level.

Economists have studied the disincentive effects of welfare payments by observing the labor market behavior of recipients in ordinary welfare programs and in massive social experiments in which thousands of families participated in alternative welfare schemes. These studies have been recently surveyed by Gary Burtless in the *Journal of Economic Perspectives* (Winter 1990) and by Robert Moffitt in the *Journal of Economic Literature* (March 1992). Studies generally have found that the disincentive effects of welfare programs are significant but small. For example, Burtless concludes that an increase in welfare benefits that increased a poor family's income by ten percent would likely reduce their labor supply by about one percent.

Current public assistance programs mostly had their origins in the 1930s, and they have grown into a complicated patchwork system whose administrative costs and benefits for recipients vary from state to state. Table 1 draws the national welfare system in its broadest outlines, showing outlays on means-tested programs (programs in which participation depends on income or wealth) in 1985.

Public assistance takes two forms. "In-kind" aid includes public housing, free medical care, or food stamps. Other programs are cash-grant programs. The best known of these is AFDC, or Aid to Families with Dependent Children. The primary aim of the AFDC program in the past has been to provide aid to single mothers with children. The figure for "other" cash assistance programs in the table above includes payments for Supplemental Security Income (SSI) and General Assistance. SSI is administered by the Social Security System and provides aid for the aged, blind, and disabled. General Assistance provides aid to families and individuals who are not eligible for benefits under AFDC or SSI. Cash transfers to the poor also take place through the Earned Income Tax Credit, which provides an earnings subsidy

Table 1 ✦ Outlays in Means-Tested Programs

Cash assistance	
AFDC	*$15.6 billion*
Other	*$17.3 billion*
In-kind assistance	
Food and nutrition	*$17.7 billion*
Housing and energy	*$12.2 billion*
Medicaid	*$41.7 billion*
TOTAL	*$104.5 billion*

Source: Burtless, op.cit., p. 59.

through the federal income tax system for poor families with children.

Since these programs are administered jointly by the federal and state governments, recipients' benefits vary widely. Table 2 shows monthly payments for a mother and two children under the AFDC program in several states in the Great Lakes region. Also shown here are the states' ranks nationwide.

Michigan's benefits shown here reflect a sharp cut in 1991. Prior to the cut, they were comparable to Wisconsin's payments. Note for purposes of comparison that Ohio's benefits are ranked at the national median level.

Wisconsin has a long record of innovative welfare reform within this system. One of the state's most successful reforms has been in the collection of child support payments. In the past, fathers who left their families often failed to provide support for their children. For example, a study in 1978 found that 57 percent of children eligible for child support payments in Wisconsin were receiving nothing. Starting in 1979, the state of Wisconsin

Table 2 ✦ Monthly Payments for a Mother and Two Children

Illinois	*$324.85*	*28th*
Indiana	*$264.00*	*39th*
Michigan	*$391.91*	*14th*
Minnesota	*$495.31*	*8th*
Ohio	*$331.63*	*26th*
Wisconsin	*$458.40*	*10th*

Source: U.S. Department of Health and Human Services, cited in Flint (Michigan) Journal, 28 April 1991.

required that child support payments be automatically withheld from the absent father's paycheck starting thirty days after falling delinquent. In 1987 the rules were changed so that child support would be withheld starting immediately after the support order was entered, and the state mandated that the absent father would pay 17 percent of his gross income for the first child, 25 percent for two children, and up to 34 percent for five or more children. These reforms have been effective: from 1985 to 1989 child support collections increased by 169 percent in Wisconsin.

The Wisconsin child support reform has been widely welcomed as an example of enlightened policy making. (Its chief critics have been—not surprisingly—absent fathers and their second wives.) The federal government adopted Wisconsin's earliest child support reforms in 1984, and Republican Governor John Engler of Michigan proposed similar reforms (coupled with the threat of revocation of the absent father's drivers license if he fails to comply) in 1992.

The federal government took steps to circumvent the disincentive effects of welfare programs as early as 1971 by requiring able-bodied recipients to obtain work-related education or training and to search for work. Programs requiring welfare recipients to work in order to continue receiving benefits have come to be known as "workfare" programs. Under its Republican governor, Tommy G. Thompson, Wisconsin introduced its own "workfare" initiatives in 1987. These were embodied in the Work Experience Job Training Program, which provided education aid and day care services to AFDC recipients, and the Community Work Experience Program, which funded public service jobs for welfare recipients.

Once again, the Wisconsin workfare reforms have provided a model for others. The reforms proposed by Michigan's Governor Engler in 1992 included workfare components. But evidence on the impact of workfare has been mixed. Governor Thompson's administration pointed to declines in the number of people receiving AFDC payments in Wisconsin (while the welfare rolls in almost all other states were growing) as evidence that workfare was a success. But a study completed by the Employment and Training Institute at the University of Wisconsin–Milwaukee in 1992 found that the percentage of workfare participants who got off welfare was approximately equal to the percentage of nonparticipants who got off welfare. The study concluded that many people left the welfare rolls in the study period, from 1987 to 1989, because the state's economy was growing, but that the workfare program seems to have had no significant impact. These results of course were not welcomed by the governor's administration, whose spokesmen accused the researchers of distorting the facts for partisan purposes.

Governor Thompson's "learnfare" program, created in 1988, has been even more controversial and harder to defend on the basis of the evidence. The aim of the learnfare program was to encourage children in welfare families to attend school more regularly. The program provides an incentive for this by threatening to reduce families' AFDC benefits by $77 per month—about fifteen percent—if a teenage family member habitually misses school. If teenage mothers receiving AFDC payments do not return to school, they lose $200 per month. In 1993 Governor Thompson proposed an expansion of the learnfare program to catch more truant students, doubling the number of families suffering benefit cuts at first, and subjecting students as young as six years old to the program's vigilance.

As in the case of the workfare program, learnfare's effects have been called into question by an early empirical study. An evaluation by the University of Wisconsin-Milwaukee's Employment and Training Institute found no evidence that learnfare had improved the attendance record of students. After one year, one-third of participating students had improved their attendance, but the attendance of more than half the students was worse. The learnfare program seemingly had not put a dent in a trend toward increases in school absences among Milwaukee high school students. It also had been plagued by record keeping problems in schools that made it difficult to verify students' attendance records.

In spite of the mixed early results achieved by learnfare, it has been popular with the public and has broadened Governor Thompson's reputation as a tough welfare innovator. The program has much in common with some of Bill Clinton's welfare reforms when he was governor of Arkansas, but President Clinton has condemned learnfare as a "failed social experiment" on the basis of the University of Wisconsin–Milwaukee's study.

In 1991 Governor Thompson presented his Parental and Family Responsibility plan, which would provide incentives for a teenage mother to marry her child's father and to limit the number of children she has. The welfare system has traditionally given more generous support to a mother if she is single, so welfare fathers have had an incentive to leave their families. Thompson proposed instead to include the teenage father in the welfare grant and pay the mother an additional $77 per month if the parents married. Thompson said this would simply encourage teenage fathers to shoulder more responsibility, but critics—who coined the label "bridefare"—pointed out that teenage marriages tend to be unstable and short-lived, and thus not a good aim for state incentives. Some suggested that encouraging marriages between ill-matched teens could increase the incidence of child abuse. Even the Wisconsin Catholic Conference, after some hesitation, decided to oppose Thompson's initiative.

Before bridefare the law granted an unmarried woman $100 more per month for each additional child. Governor Thompson claimed that this led women to have more children in order to increase their welfare checks. Under his Parental and Family Responsibility proposal, the size of an unmarried mother's grant would rise by only half as much for a second child and not rise at all for any additional children. This aspect of bridefare has also elicited strong reactions from critics, the most extreme of which suggest that limits on welfare payments for additional children might raise abortion rates.

In recent years the states have been viewed as laboratories in which reform experiments such as Wisconsin's can be tested. Since about half the funding for a state's AFDC program comes from the federal government, welfare reform proposals must gain federal approval. Wisconsin's bridefare program was submitted for federal approval in 1992. Since it was a popular Republican governor's program, it gave the Bush administration an opportunity to promote his party's platform at the beginning of an election year. Cutting through the usual red tape, federal authorities approved the program in a record 24 days.

Since gaining federal approval for the bridefare plan, Wisconsin has been running the program on a trial basis in four counties, including Milwaukee. It is too early to judge its success.

Michigan's welfare reform efforts were spurred by budgetary problems during the 1990-91 recession. Facing a budget deficit projected at $1 billion, Republican Governor John Engler stopped general assistance payments to 83,000 able-bodied recipients on October 1, 1991, thus saving about $200 million per year. At the time Michigan's unemployment rate was over 9 percent, the highest in the nation, so it was difficult for those affected to find jobs. A report released by the state's Department of Social Services and the University of Michigan School of Social Work in March 1992 found that few of those dropped from general assistance were working. Six percent had shifted to other public assistance programs that actually paid more; 83 percent were receiving health or food aid from the state, but no cash assistance; and 10 percent were receiving no state help.

Governor Engler regained some measure of approval from his critics in 1992 when he proposed a broader program of welfare reforms. His proposals included several ideas, such as workfare, learnfare, and tighter enforcement of child-support laws, that mirrored Wisconsin initiatives. He also proposed to allow more two-parent families to receive welfare payments and to let welfare families keep a larger share of their earnings from work. The latter would represent a reduction in the welfare system's implicit tax on earnings, thus cutting the work disincentives implicit in the welfare system.

GARBAGE ECONOMICS

Wayne Carroll

University of Wisconsin-Eau Claire

In small towns in the Midwest, life used to be simpler. At least that's how it looks in the stories passed down from older generations. Most people recognize those small towns when they're portrayed in movies, with small shops ringing the town square and tidy homes surrounded by picket fences just a couple of blocks away. But let the imagination wander a little outside town, and one may come upon another facet of the simple life: the town dump. A small town's trash might have been dumped in a clearing, with the surrounding trees catching some of the paper lifted from the pile by a stiff breeze. The town dump might have been administered by the local refuse hauler or by a sand and gravel business that owned the land.

Life may never have really been that simple before, but it is certain that it's not simple now. Even trash is getting complicated. Trash collection charges are rising, and in many communities residents can no longer throw grass clippings, newspapers, or soda cans in the garbage can. Today it pays to learn to recognize quickly the difference between #1 plastic (polyethylene terephthalate) and #2 plastic (high-density polyethylene); and those who are truly politically correct use stationery with at least 75 percent post-consumer content. Solid waste issues, while still not as important as peace in the Middle East or AIDS, now receive our attention and efforts.

Current levels of awareness of solid waste problems date back to the 1960s and 1970s. Growing awareness of groundwater pollution problems and the dangers of toxic substances in the waste stream brought a realization that the town dumps and sanitary landfills of old were not as harmless as they appeared. Congress expressed this growing concern when it passed the Resource Conservation and Recovery Act (RCRA) in 1976, which directed the Environmental Protection Agency (EPA) to establish more stringent standards governing landfills. Operators of landfills that accept household solid waste now are required to provide clay liners under the landfill; provide drainage for "leachate," the possibly toxic liquids that leach out of the landfill; cover the landfill daily; and test neighboring groundwater flows for pollution. These precautions are expensive and have driven the old-fashioned town dump out of business. Henceforth landfills will be "engineered," meeting the most advanced technical standards.

Change always creates opportunities for profit. RCRA brought fundamental change to the solid waste disposal industry; subsequently entrepreneurs have sought to profit from the opportunities it created, and government authorities have tried to shape the emerging institutions.

In the crowded metropolitan areas of the East Coast, landfill space is relatively scarce, so waste disposal is more costly than in many other parts of the country. Trash and recycling haulers have taken advantage of the regional differences in disposal costs by transporting East Coast trash to cheaper landfills in the Midwest. In 1990, 21 percent of New Jersey's trash was shipped out of the state for disposal. Most went to Pennsylvania, but large shares also went to Kentucky and Ohio. A smaller quantity went to Indiana, but these shipments became a hot political issue in 1990 and 1991. Senator Dan Coats, an Indiana Republican, protested the trash imports in his campaign by airing television ads showing a man dressed as a New Jersey garbage collector dumping a sack full of trash on the porch of an Indiana home. In 1991 it was discovered that the haulers transporting trash from New Jersey had circumvented New Jersey's legal waste disposal requirements in order to avoid paying processing charges there. The states of Indiana and New Jersey entered into a pact in 1991 in which they agreed to share information about the origins of such trash shipments so Indiana officials could recognize and turn back those that were illegal. While this issue was resolved to the satisfaction of officials in both states, a thorny underlying issue deserves some thought: whose interests are served by efforts to discourage interregional solid waste shipments?

Indiana was not alone in its concern about imports of solid waste filling its landfills. After Ohio accepted 3.7 million tons of other states' trash in 1989 and 1.9 million tons in 1990 (much of it going to Ohio's trash-burning incinerators), Ohio Governor George Voinovich asked his state's landfill operators to voluntarily stop accepting trash from elsewhere. In July 1992, a half-mile-long freight train carrying trash from New York City wandered through Illinois in search of a disposal site. Leachate leaked from some of the rail cars and one boxcar caught fire as it passed through Illinois to an uncertain destination. And officials in Wisconsin noted that waste haulers from Illinois dumped more trash in Wisconsin than was generated in the entire city of Milwaukee in 1992. Ninety-three percent of the waste imported into Wisconsin came from Illinois, and most of the rest came from Minnesota. But Wisconsin landfills also accepted waste from Indiana, Michigan, Iowa, Kansas, and Maryland. The Wisconsin Department of Natural Resources recently approved new landfill regulations that will effectively slow the flow of imports of municipal solid waste into the state, since any parties disposing of waste in Wisconsin landfills will be required to have prior certification from the DNR.

The demands made by RCRA and other stringent landfill standards have placed a premium on technical expertise in landfill design and operation, so private-sector firms that specialize in this field have begun to open large-scale landfills that can supplant the current generation of landfills, which are more often publicly administered. New landfills often cross jurisdictional lines, and private firms can more easily negotiate the bureaucratic obstacles involved in landfill siting. Thus in the future municipal solid waste is more likely to be transported to a regional, privately operated landfill for disposal. The concentration of a region's landfill capacity in the hands of a single private operator raises the possibility of monopolistic pricing of landfill services, but the greater efficiency of private operators might outweigh this.

As the costs of landfill space rise in step with the government's technical requirements, alternative modes of waste disposal—source reduction, incineration, and recycling—look relatively more attractive. "Source reduction" refers to efforts by producers or consumers to reduce the amount of waste they generate by adopting more careful (and more costly) production techniques or consumption habits.

Incineration (or burning) of trash has been controversial in recent years. Proponents have built massive incinerators that can turn a large share of a metropolitan area's solid waste into a more compact, inert ash, which is subsequently landfilled. Most of these units generate electricity from trash. Hazardous (or toxic) wastes can often be eliminated more safely in an incinerator than in a landfill, since the high temperatures at which an incinerator operates tend to render toxic substances harmless. Old tires are highly combustible, and fires in tire dumps are hard to control; but the energy content of tires make them a potent fuel in a waste-to-energy plant.

Minnesota has used incineration more than most states. In 1991 there were twelve garbage burners in the state, including one in downtown Minneapolis, and they burned 30 percent of the state's municipal solid waste. The state relies so heavily on incinerators because government leaders there recognized in the early 1980s that leaking landfills presented serious environmental problems, and at that time incinerators appeared to be a safe, clean alternative.

However, critics have subsequently raised questions about the safety of incinerators. When municipal solid waste or hazardous waste are burned, low levels of toxic pollutants can escape into the air, and traces of toxic substances can remain in the incinerator ash that is sent to the landfill.

The debate over the safety of incinerators has raged for twelve years in East Liverpool, Ohio, located on the Ohio River some thirty miles downstream from Pittsburgh. Waste Technologies Industries built a $160 million hazardous waste incinerator there and has fought a long series of legal battles to gain permission to begin operations. Many local residents support the firm's efforts to operate the plant, perhaps because it will eventually employ over 200 workers in a town where jobs are scarce. The plant has been opposed by environmental groups, the governor and attorney general of nearby West Virginia, actor Martin Sheen, and many others. On December 7, 1992, newly elected vice-president Al Gore vowed that a final test burn would be delayed until after the federal government could further investigate the possibility of dioxin contamination from the plant's emissions, but the EPA and a federal appeals court ruled that the East Liverpool plant could begin operations.

Since the environmental safety of incinerators is so uncertain, efforts to conserve landfill space have focused on recycling. It is conceivable that recycling could be handled by the private sector. If high landfill costs were passed on to households and businesses in the form of higher trash collection costs, they would have an incentive to seek alternative means of disposing of their trash. Private firms could provide recycling services at prices set by the market, paying for valuable recyclable materials such as aluminum cans and charging for pickup of others.

But responsibility for recycling has been largely taken over by government authorities. Most states will soon require communities to offer recycling services, and these services usually will be provided by municipal agencies or by haulers with exclusive contracts with their communities. The seeming failure of the private sector to handle the recycling business can be attributed in part to the fact that communities often subsidize landfill operations, so the "tipping fee" charged when trash is dumped at the landfill is set below the true cost of landfill space. This subsidy is passed on to households and businesses in relatively low trash collection charges, so they have little incentive to reduce their waste flow or to recycle their waste. Since government authorities wish to reduce the amount of trash dumped at the landfill in order to extend the landfill's operating life, they must prohibit landfill disposal of certain recyclable materials and require that they be recycled.

For example, the state of Wisconsin has prohibited landfill disposal of newspapers, aluminum and steel cans, some plastics, grass clippings, and some other materials after 1995 and will require communities to establish recycling programs that meet stringent state performance standards. Almost all communities in the state will provide recycling as a municipal service or a public monopoly. The notable exception is the city of Eau Claire, in which households can choose to buy recycling services from one of several trash-hauling firms or to haul their recyclables to rural drop-off sites operated by the county. When Eau Claire's recycling program began in early 1992, there were only a few firms offering curbside recycling pickup, and at $5 per month their fee was about twice as high as the per-household cost of recycling in other communities. After about a year, new firms entered the market, and the monthly fee paid by many households dropped to $3. It is likely that recycling services in Eau Claire will remain somewhat more expensive than similar services in other communities, because the larger number of haulers in Eau Claire makes it impossible to realize scale economies that are achieved elsewhere.

In the eyes of the public, these changes are facets of the "garbage crisis," the apparent shortage of landfill space, that has loomed large since the passage of RCRA. Economists tend to discount worries about such crises. Economists pointed out that the shortages that marked the "energy crisis" of the 1970s and early 1980s were due to price controls on gasoline and natural gas rather than some impending catastrophe; and in any case the higher oil and gasoline prices that prevailed at that time created incentives for dramatic energy-saving adjustments through the workings of normal market forces. It is thus not surprising that the "garbage crisis" is proving to be less earth-shaking than many expected.

While the increases in landfill costs in the 1980s were large and unprecedented, forecasts of skyrocketing future costs proved to have been too alarmist. Local governments that built waste-to-energy incinerators in the early 1980s built them with large capacities in anticipation of heavy demands in the near future. Government authorities often entered into an agreement with the private operators of an incinerator in which they guaranteed that at least a specified minimum quantity of trash would be hauled to the incinerator to be consumed as fuel. They also guaranteed that the incinerator operator could charge tipping fees that, while high by the standards of the 1980s, were expected to be a bargain in the long run as landfill charges rose. This would assure the operators that they could earn a steady flow of revenue from their tipping fees and from sales of the electricity they produced. The local government might then require all trash collectors within its jurisdiction to haul their trash to the incinerator in order to achieve the guaranteed flow of solid waste. Requirements of this sort, which are called "flow control," shifted the risk of financial losses from the private operators to the government and were deemed necessary in order to induce the private operators to invest in the trash-burning plants in the first place.

But in the early 1990s the flow of solid waste into landfills and incinerators was smaller than expected due to the national economic recession and the diversion of some waste into growing recycling programs. One consequence has been that landfill charges have not risen as quickly as anticipated. In fact, the county landfill in Eau Claire, Wisconsin, reduced its tipping fee in 1990 in order to attract *more* trash, since the county board realized that its tipping fee revenue was falling short of expectations. Since landfill charges have stayed lower than expected, they generally have remained lower than the tipping fees charged by incinerators. According to a recent *Wall Street Journal* article (11 August 1993), the average incinerator tipping fee (or trash disposal charge) is $56 per ton, while the average landfill tipping fee is only $28 per ton. Thus trash collectors have an incentive to haul trash to landfills rather than incinerators, making enforcement of flow control restrictions difficult. For example, authorities in Columbus, Ohio, estimated that 15 percent of the solid waste that haulers were required to deliver to the regional incinerator was being diverted to cheaper destinations such as nearby landfills.

In spite of flow control, the quantities of waste delivered to incinerators have often fallen far short of the guaranteed levels, so local governments have been forced to take drastic steps to keep their commitments to the incinerator operators. An incinerator in Claremont, New Hampshire, charges local trash haulers a tipping fee of $96.50 per ton, but in order to attract a larger flow of fuel it only charges $40 per ton for trash imported from elsewhere. Columbus, Ohio, kept its incinerator's tipping fees low to match a local landfill's charges, but this required over $100 million in subsidies in ten years. Columbus has recently opted instead to charge a higher fee and enforce flow control restrictions more effectively. County officials in La Crosse, Wisconsin, sued their engineering consultants for $2.6 million for overestimating the flow of trash that would be generated in the area to feed its incinerator.

PROPERTY TAX REFORM

Wayne Carroll

University of Wisconsin-Eau Claire

In Boston, the owner of a $100,000 home pays about $850 per year in property taxes. By contrast, the owner of a $100,000 home in Eau Claire, Wisconsin, pays over $3,000 per year in property taxes. The relatively high property taxes in Eau Claire are typical of those paid in other jurisdictions in Wisconsin and in other states in the Upper Midwest. Given this heavy property tax burden, it is not surprising that there has been strong support for efforts to cut property taxes sharply in these states. In fact, property tax reform efforts have been one of the hottest political issues in the Upper Midwest in the last twenty years.

Table 1 on page 38 shows how each of six states in this region ranked relative to other states in their per capita state and local tax burden and their per capita property tax burden in 1988. (The phrase "from own sources" in the table means that these figures ignore revenue transferred to the states from the federal government.)

Three of these states—Michigan, Minnesota, and Wisconsin—clearly stand above the national average in their per capita state and local tax burden, and Illinois joins them near the top of the rankings in property tax burden. (The states ranked higher than these nationally are mostly in the Northeast.)

Why are taxes high in those states? The heavy tax burdens in Michigan, Minnesota, and Wisconsin reflect strong commitments in these states to spending on various government services. Table 2 shows rankings of these

Table 1 ✦ Per Capita Taxes

	total revenue from own sources	property tax revenue
Illinois	*28th*	*17th*
Indiana	*40th*	*30th*
Michigan	*13th*	*10th*
Minnesota	*5th*	*18th*
Ohio	*35th*	*31st*
Wisconsin	*17th*	*14th*

Source: Department of Commerce, Bureau of the Census; cited in *Facts and Figures on Government Finance,* 1991 edition, p.188.

states in their per capita expenditures in several categories. Once again Michigan, Minnesota, and Wisconsin rank near the top in many categories.

Taxes are levied at three levels: federal, state, and local. "Local" authorities include cities, counties, school districts, and districts created to fund other functions. Generally speaking, property taxes are the main revenue source for local governments, accounting for about one-half of local government revenue in recent years. Property tax payments by owners of commercial and industrial property make up about one-half of total property tax revenue; homeowners' payments contribute another one third of the total; and owners of rental properties pay the remainder.

The annual property tax payment made by a property owner is equal to a

Table 2 ✦ Per Capita Expenditures

	total	education	highways	public welfare	health, hospitals
Illinois	*28th*	*37th*	*27th*	*17th*	*41st*
Indiana	*41st*	*28th*	*47th*	*28th*	*22nd*
Michigan	*11th*	*6th*	*45th*	*8th*	*8th*
Minnesota	*5th*	*7th*	*8th*	*5th*	*13th*
Ohio	*31st*	*31st*	*46th*	*11th*	*29th*
Wisconsin	*17th*	*8th*	*25th*	*7th*	*36th*

Source: Department of Commerce, Bureau of the Census; cited in *Facts and Figures,* p. 174.

specified percentage (the tax rate) of the assessed valuation of the property. Local governments conventionally assess property at a value lower than its true market value. Although assessment conventions differ across communities, property taxes can be compared across jurisdictions by expressing tax rates as a percentage of the true market value. For example, the assessed values of homes in a community might be ninety percent of their true market value. Then if the tax rate is $10 per thousand dollars of assessed valuation, the true tax rate is $9 per thousand dollars of market value.

The owner of a $100,000 home in Eau Claire, Wisconsin, would see the following charges on the annual property tax statement in 1993:

county	*$498.60*
city	*$784.13*
school district	*$2183.65*
vocational-technical college	*$200.32*
TOTAL	*$3666.70*

(These figures take into account some property tax relief payments from the state.) Property taxes in bigger cities fund a broad range of services. For example, property taxes in Milwaukee county fund schools, social service, and welfare programs in the city of Milwaukee, the airport, County Stadium (the home of the Milwaukee Brewers baseball team), and many cultural amenities downtown.

The burden of high residential property taxes in a community such as Eau Claire seems reason enough to call for cuts, but the public antipathy to property taxes runs deeper than this and extends across the nation. The opposition to property taxes can be attributed in part to two perceived evils: their inequity and regressivity.

Property taxes appear to be inequitable for many reasons. Property tax payments can constitute a large share of a poor family's income. In addition, an affluent community with high property values can generate greater property tax revenue than a less affluent community with comparable tax rates. The affluent community might choose to levy property taxes at lower rates, exploiting its higher tax base to generate substantial revenue. This would provide an incentive for businesses to locate in affluent communities in order to take advantage of the lower tax rates, thus widening the difference in property values between rich and poor communities.

Years ago the Minnesota state legislature took steps to address problems of inequity in the property tax structure by setting tax rates on low-valued homes below the rates on higher-valued homes, apartment buildings, or businesses in order to offer assistance to lower-income homeowners. In particular, in 1991 the tax rate on homes was one percent of the value up to $68,000, two percent of the next $42,000 in value, and three percent of the value in excess of $110,000. Large businesses were taxed at almost five percent, and apartments were taxed at 3.6 percent. While the residential property tax rates are lower than in some other states, Minnesota's business property tax rates are among the nation's highest.

These differential rates certainly help low-income citizens in Minnesota, but many in the state, particularly in the business community and among homeowners in affluent suburbs, see the differences in rates as inequitable. Minnesota's Republican governor, Arne Carlson, proposed in 1991 to realign these rates, taxing all homes and apartments at a rate of two percent and businesses at a rate of four percent. Since this would double the property tax burden for many of Minnesota's poorest homeowners while providing large cuts for owners of expensive homes and large businesses, the proposal was dead on arrival in the state legislature. But the political pressures for property tax reforms along these lines will surely persist in Minnesota as the state tries to find a consensus on what constitutes "equity."

Alternatively an affluent community could set tax rates higher to obtain generous funding to support superior schools and other services. In fact, some defenders of property taxes argue that this is a virtue, since it allows people to choose to live either in high-tax, high-service communities or in other communities with low taxes and modest services.

But differences between communities in levels of services or quality of schools are narrowed by state subsidies to poorer districts. The state of Minnesota sends generous state aid to outstate cities, where property values and incomes are typically lower. For example, $1.5 million in state aid allowed Hibbing to spend $2.7 million more than suburban New Hope, even though property tax payments in Hibbing were $1 million less. The state of Wisconsin employs a rather complicated formula to allocate state funds among school districts in order to equalize their ability to fund public schooling.

Most studies have concluded that property taxes are regressive; that is, property tax payments generally take a larger share of income in lower-income families than in higher-income families. Evaluating the evidence on this is not as simple as it might appear. For example, consider a family whose average income in the long run is at the median level for the population. Suppose that in one year this family falls on hard times (due to a temporary slump in the family business, for example), but that the family correctly anticipates that its fortunes will improve later. Such a family will likely own a moderately large home and pay property taxes near the median level, but a

Table 3 ✦ State and Local Tax Sources

	income taxes	sales taxes	property taxes	other taxes
Michigan	33.4	16.8	38.0	11.8
Minnesota	34.0	18.9	30.0	17.1
Wisconsin	30.3	19.4	35.2	15.1

Source: Department of Commerce, Bureau of the Census; cited in *Facts and Figures,* p.198.

study undertaken in the year when their income is lower will identify them simply as a lower-income family that pays relatively high property taxes. Since data collected at any point in time will invariably include such cases, studies tend to overstate the regressivity of the property tax. However, economists who have addressed this problem generally agree that the evidence would show that the property tax is regressive even if this problem (and others of this sort) were eliminated.

There is strong sentiment for cuts in property tax revenues, but obviously a cut cannot be painless. Holding other things constant, it must be accompanied by either an increase in revenues from another source or a cut in local government services.

Consider the first alternative. If property taxes are cut, the revenue lost by local taxing authorities can be replaced by funds from other local sources such as user fees for water service, garbage service, or sewer service; or from state sources such as state income taxes, lottery proceeds, retail sales taxes, or taxes on services.

The effects of a shift of this sort can be seen in Table 1 by comparing Minnesota with either Michigan or Wisconsin. Minnesota's overall per capita tax burden is greater (ranking the state fifth in the nation), but its ranking in per capita property taxes is considerably lower. This reflects the lasting impact of an effort by the Minnesota state legislature starting in 1972 to shift the tax burden from property taxes to other sources. Table 3 shows what percentages of state and local tax collections came from various sources in these states in 1988.

Minnesota relies significantly less heavily on the property tax than the other two states. It has replaced that property tax revenue by collecting more in income taxes (compared with Wisconsin) and more in sales taxes and other taxes (compared with Michigan).

The second alternative to high property taxes is a cut in local government services. As communities across the nation attempt to cut their local tax burdens, funding for libraries, schools, road maintenance, and other services may be cut sharply. Since the 1970s there has been strong sentiment in many states for reductions in the size and importance of government in order to eliminate wasteful spending. Cuts in property tax revenue can be the carrot that leads the electorate to budget cuts.

In 1978 voters in California struck an historic blow against property taxes when they approved Proposition 13 in a referendum. Property values had risen sharply in the preceding years, with assessed valuations and property tax bills following in lockstep fashion. Proposition 13 placed a ceiling on annual increases in property assessments and limited property tax rates to a maximum of one percent of a property's assessed valuation, thereby reducing property tax revenue by about $7 billion after one year and dropping it from 50 percent above the national average to 35 percent below the national average. Ten years later California ranked tenth among states in its per capita state and local government expenditures, but this high ranking was due in part to the state's higher-than-average income levels. California's ratio of state and local spending to personal income ranked only 30th in the nation in 1988, compared with ranks of 16th in Michigan, 9th in Minnesota, and 18th in Wisconsin.

Thus it appears that Proposition 13 and other accompanying tax reform measures in California have indeed significantly cut state and local government spending. Spending has been cut in the areas of government administration, health services, parks and recreation, and libraries, while police and fire protection and other "essential" services now take larger shares of total spending. Proposition 13 has also led local government authorities in California to turn to alternative revenue sources such as state funds and local user fees.

Today almost all states place limits of some sort on property taxes. Most states limit the annual growth in the tax burden to a maximum percentage and allow overrides only by approval of the voters. While the nature of the tax limitation schemes varies from state to state, there is evidence that these measures generally have not reduced state and local government spending below the level it would have achieved otherwise. But it is clear that these states have been successful in shifting their tax burden away from property taxes.

Wisconsin is one of the few states that has not adopted limits on property tax rates. In fact, the fiscal rules established by the state guarantee a prominent role for property taxes in local finance. While the state has set no legal limit on property tax rates, it allows local governments to tap only a narrow set of alternative funding sources (such as optional county sales taxes). Virtually the only recourse for those seeking an alternative to the property tax is to press for property tax relief from the state. As a result, debates on the merits of alternative tax relief plans are a perennial feature in Madison.

Property taxes fall particularly heavily on farmers in Michigan and Wisconsin. Excluding northeastern states, where farm property values and tax payments are the nation's highest, Michigan had the highest per-acre farm property taxes in 1990, and Wisconsin ranked third, according to the Wisconsin Agriculture Department. Michigan's property taxes were an average of $33.18 per acre and Wisconsin's were $17.18 per acre, compared with $10.94 in Iowa, $8.11 in Indiana, and only $6.90 per acre in Minnesota.

Wisconsin farmers benefit from a number of property tax relief programs, but their tax payments have risen steadily over the last several years as farm land values have grown and tax rates have been increased. For example, farm property tax revenue in Wisconsin grew by 31 percent from 1987 to 1991. Over this period the value of the state's farm land rose by 9 percent, with the remainder of the increase in tax revenue attributable to increases in tax rates. Like others in Wisconsin, farmers await more substantial relief from the state's high property tax burden.

ESTABLISHING A
VALUE FOR WATER

Richard Lichty

University of Minnesota–Duluth

It was only twenty to thirty years ago that many economics professors were arguing that water was not an "economic good" because water was not scarce relative to demand. Economic goods are goods that are scarce enough to command a price in a free market.

How times have changed! For the past thirty years demand for water has rapidly increased for purposes such as: a dumping site for personal and industrial wastes; a source of irrigation in what otherwise would be a desert; a source of cooling for electrical generators; a source of recreation; and a myriad of additional uses too numerous to mention.

Economists (and others) have come to realize that water is no longer a "free good." Once a resource such as water becomes "economic," choices concerning its allocation between competing ends must be made.

A free market allocates resources on the basis of a willingness and ability to pay. That is, whichever use for the resource commands the highest value in terms of satisfaction to the consumer and profits to the producer will be the use that prevails in the marketplace.

This all sounds fine. But historically, water has not been exchanged in a free and competitive market. When water becomes relatively scarce in this sense, some type of centralized allocation scheme is probably preferable to a first come, first serve allocation that represents the only other real alternative.

No private market for water currently exists in Minnesota. Yet, especially

Table 1 ✦ Water Use, Production, and Value of Production for Corn

Acre Feet of Water	Total Production of Corn (bushels)	Change in Level of Corn Production	Price of Corn	Value of Additional Corn in Revenues
0	0		4	
1	10	10	4	40
2	18	8	4	36
3	24	6	4	24
4	28	4	4	16
5	30	2	4	8
6	30	0	4	0

in the Twin Cities of Minneapolis and St. Paul, water shortages can occur and allocations may well need to be made. In this context, Minnesota contracted with the University of Minnesota to establish value estimates for water in alternative uses. The purpose of this research program was to establish a basis for allocating water that would mirror the result that would be obtained from a free market, i.e., an allocation so as to maximize the total value from the use of the state's water resources.

Before reviewing the conclusions of the Minnesota study, it is probably worthwhile to discuss the words "value" and "efficiency" relative to a functioning market. The easiest way to say it is that efficiency means maximizing some kind of output given the inputs or minimizing the use of inputs given an output. The relative values of inputs depend upon what one is trying to maximize.

This means that there are many types of efficiencies, in this case the notion of market efficiency. Suppose someone has two uses for water; irrigation for corn and water for cattle. Suppose further that the relationships shown in Tables 1 and 2 exist between water, production, and prices for these two possible uses.

As can be seen from these two tables, the value of the use of water stems from the value of production coming out of the water use. Assuming that the amount and fertility of land, the amount and quality of labor, and the amount and quality of machinery are all constant, all changes in production of corn and cattle can be attributed only to changes in the amount of water used. Therefore, the additional revenues earned are measures of the value of water's contribution to production.

Notice also that the production of corn and of cattle follow the well

Table 2 ✦ Water Use, Production, and Value of Production for Cattle

Acre Feet of Water	Total Production of Cattle	Change in Level of Cattle Production	Price of Cattle	Value of Additional Cattle in Revenues
0	0		15	
1	3	3	15	45
2	5	2	15	30
3	6	1	15	15
4	6	0	15	0

known "law of diminishing returns" which states, "As more and more units of a variable resource are added to other resources whose supplies are fixed, output will increase, but at a diminishing rate". Thus, the changes in the amount of both corn and cattle produced decrease with increasing inputs of water, holding the amounts and qualities of other resource inputs constant.

There is no allocation problem if there are eight or more acre feet of water available to these two uses. Value is a meaningless concept unless there is scarcity. Under this scenario of plenty, the corn farmer would produce thirty bushels of corn and the cattle producer would produce six cattle. The total value from the production of these two commodities would be equal to 214 (40+36+24+16+8+45+30+15).

But what if there are only five acre feet of water available? What would be the efficient allocation? Well, a free market would allocate the water to whomever would be willing and able to pay the most for it. Who could afford to pay the most for the first acre foot?

The cattle producers earn a revenue of $45 from the first acre foot by producing three cows while the corn producers only earn $40 from that same acre foot by producing ten bushels. Clearly the cattle producers can out-bid the corn producers (up to $5) for that first acre foot.

What about the second acre foot? The second acre foot could either add $30 to the cattle producer's revenues or $40 to the corn producer's revenues. So now the corn producers have the advantage to the tune of a $10 difference.

The third acre foot would go to the corn producers ($36 in revenues vs. $30 for the cattle producers). The fourth acre foot would go to the cattle producers ($30 in revenues versus $24 for the corn producers). The final (fifth) acre foot would go to the corn producers ($24 in revenues versus $15 for the cattle producers).

As things turn out, the five acre feet would allow the corn producers to produce twenty-four bushels of corn and the cattle producers to produce five cows. What is more important, the total value of production in the economy will have been maximized! There would be no other allocation of water that could increase total value.

To see this, suppose the fifth acre foot of water is taken out of corn production and put it into cattle production. The economy will lose $24 in value from the corn production but only gain $15 in value from cattle production, a net loss of $9 in agricultural production. The same type of loss would occur if the fourth acre foot of water is taken out of cattle production and put it into corn production.

If any change made is a net loss, then production must be at the best position possible. In fact, a free market where the one earning the most revenues can outbid all others for the use of a resource, in this case water, will automatically allocate resources so as to maximize the value of society's production.

So, what is value? It is based on consumers' willingness and ability to pay for additional production. What is efficiency? In a market context, it is the maximization of total value coming out of a given allocation of a particular resource between productive alternatives. That is, because total value is maximized with an allocation of three acre feet to corn production and two acre feet to cattle production, that allocation is said to be *efficient*.

When economists refer to "efficiency" they are almost always speaking in terms of market efficiency. However, market efficiency is only one of many maximization possibilities. In this context, value is a relative concept that depends on the objective being maximized. The concept of value for market efficiency is based on a "willingness and ability to pay" for a given resource.

Economists are excited about this form of value (and efficiency) because if markets are working perfectly values will be determined in such a way that efficiency will be brought about automatically without any needed interference from government. There is no chance for governmental (bureaucratic) mess-ups if the market is functioning properly.

Society might have objectives other than market efficiency, however. Some possibilities include: Maximizing the economy's rate of economic expansion (growth), maximizing the economy's level of employment, maximizing the economy's level of production (output), maximizing the economy's income level, maximizing the economy's tax base, or even bringing about a maximum level of equity (equality) out of alternative resource allocations. The notion of value would change with a choice of any one of these objective alternatives.

For example, if the goal were to maximize the economy's level of employment, water would be allocated to corn production or to cattle production based on each acre foot's contribution to jobs created rather than on each acre foot's contribution to a firm's revenues. We would need two new tables (in addition to Tables 1 and 2) with a ranking of the extra employees needed as a result of each acre foot of water allocated to establish the most "efficient" allocation of the five acre feet under this new arrangement. The same general rules apply to the other efficiency criteria listed above.

Which of the efficiency criteria should be choosen is a societal value judgement. If society chooses a laissez faire free enterprise system, it is also opting for the market efficiency criterion. If society chooses one of the other possibilities, it might very well be opting for some kind of mixed or planned economic system.

The point is, there are no right or wrong criteria selections. There are only choices to be made. Once the criterion to pursue is decided, the definition of value and the resulting efficiency criteria follow in a logical pattern.

It has already been mentioned that many states like Minnesota do not have a market system in place for the allocation of water. Therefore, when it appears water might become scarce relative to demands, some kind of allocation scheme needs to be designed that is efficient in terms of specified objectives.

The University of Minnesota entered into a contract with the state of Minnesota to evaluate the value of water under several objective criteria. What follows are some of the concerns, criteria, and methods used for water valuation estimation.

The tool employed in this analysis is known as input-output. The student does not need to know the details of such models to gain an appreciation for how they might be used.

Input-output simply traces through the structure of an economy by looking at identified regional industrial sector sales to and purchases from one another. For example, let's say that the cattle industry produces $90 worth of output. In order to do so, the industry must purchase "intermediate inputs" from other industries inside and outside of the region.

Perhaps one of the cattle farmers needs a fence. So, he or she goes to the local lumberyard (and fence supplier) and buys a fence. In doing so, he or she forces the lumber yard to hire some workers (salespeople, fence deliverers, and so on). He or she also provides the local lumberyard owner with some income.

Now suppose the farmer needs some seeds. He goes to the local feed store and purchases some seed. The feed store needs to hire some labor to service this need as well.

In addition to any labor hired by the farmer, two stores in town have to provide employment so the farmer's intermediate needs are met. In this way, the farmer's output translates into direct jobs on the farm and in the local stores.

But this is not the end of the story. In order for the lumberyard to operate, it needs the accounting services from the local CPA firm. The CPA firm hires accountants, secretaries, and custodians in order to provide its services. It also purchases the services of the local law firm.

The local law firm hires its lawyers, secretaries, and custodians and purchases intermediate products from the local office supply store. The office supply store . . . and so on.

Purchases from the local farmers ripple through the economy, each firm requiring labor and supplies from other local firms. The final result is a multiplied round of employment, direct from the farm and its direct suppliers and indirect from the second round of accountants, attorneys, and office supply stores and their employees.

What has all this to do with the value of water? The more water allocated to the cattle producers, the more employment is created via the scenario drawn immediately above. In other words, if there were only five acre feet available, allocating this water to cattle production produces a particular pattern of employment growth in the region.

Of course, the corn farmers have their own pattern of employment generation that is probably somewhat different from the cattle farmer's. Any water allocated to the corn farmers provides another pattern of employment growth in the region.

Where should the first acre foot of water go? To the industry providing the most direct and indirect employment for that acre foot. Where should the second acre foot go? To the industry providing the second most direct and indirect employment from this additional water. And so the process goes until all acre feet are allocated.

We are trying to maximize employment in this particular example. We could do the same for output or income. The point is that such allocations of water are efficient when they maximize the value of the chosen variable—employment, output, or income. This is obviously a different form of efficiency than the market efficiency described earlier.

The primary strength the interindustry approach (utilizing input-output analysis) brings to the estimation of resource values is that such an approach looks at interdependencies within a regional economy. Without taking regional structure into account, water would simply be allocated to whichever industry has the highest direct output, employment, or income associated with it (depending on which objective being maximized).

Think about the structure of a local economy. There are three ways in which an industry could impact a region. It could be quite big in and of itself (have the greatest level of output, employment, etc.) but not interact much with the local economy. Or it could be a relatively small industry but purchase most of its intermediate products locally and/or sell much of its output locally. Or finally, it could be some other combination of these two possibilities.

A relatively small firm that strongly interacts with other local firms could conceivably exert a larger total impact on the local economy than a large firm that does not depend on other local economic agents to any great extent. To allocate scarce water to the larger firm just because it is large could actually fail to maximize desired variables like employment, income, and output. The value of water for creating a desired outcome would be higher for the smaller firm and any allocation away from this firm would not be efficient.

So how does one measure value in this sense. In order to measure the value of water in various industrial uses, the social objectives for the regional economy must first be determined.

Suppose the objective is to maximize employment. One would begin by analyzing the levels of direct and indirect impacts from each of the local industries. In doing so, the ripple effects (called multiplier effects) on an industry by industry basis would be identified.

These employment ripples (multipliers) would then be compared to the direct and indirect water requirements of each industry. Industries would then be ranked according to how much direct and indirect employment is created per unit of direct and indirect water requirement. In other words, water would be allocated to those industries providing the biggest employment bang for the acre foot of water allocated.

The ratios of employment to water use multipliers represent the value of water towards employment maximization for each industry in the region in the following sense. Suppose that water is constraining the level of economic activity (in this example, employment) in the region. Now suppose suddenly X acre feet of new water has been made available. How should these new acre feet of water be allocated?

If the objective is to maximize regional employment, the new acre feet should be allocated so that the industrial sector with the highest ratio of multipliers can meet all its unfilled final demands, then to the sector with the next highest ratio so it can meet its unfilled final demands, and so on. In other words, the water should be allocated to its most highly valued uses which, in this case, are the uses that lead to the generation of the most employment in the region. Clearly the above procedure results in the greatest increase in gross regional employment per unit of water allocated. In this sense, the water allocation is efficient.

Conversely, suppose all final demands are currently being met by all sectors and that again all available supplies of water in the region are being utilized. Now assume a shortage of X acre feet of water occurs in the region. Where should the cuts in water use be made? Given the same objective of maximizing employment, those sectors with the *lowest* ratios of multipliers should be cut back first. This would insure the smallest loss of regional employment possible.

The same procedure could be used for any other economic variable (income or output for example) associated with the input-output system. The only realization necessary is that the objective variable chosen will alter the computed values of water.

The water allocation scheme for Minnesota was based on the objective of maximizing employment. The rankings in Table 3 are interpreted as follows: If there is not enough water to satisfy the production requirements to meet the state's level of final demand and if the maximization of employment is the state's objective, any additional water that might become available should be allocated first to the industry exhibiting the largest employment (direct and indirect) effects per use of one acre foot of water. Once that demand for that industry's output is satisfied (again, directly and indirectly), the next unit of new water should go to the industry exhibiting the next largest effect on employment, and so on until all new water is fully allocated. To continue such an allocation across all industries would be to maximize the employment out of a given supply of water.

In the complete study, value estimators were constructed for both ground and surface water. Only the values for surface waters will be presented here. The input-output system used for this analysis consisted of seventy-five industries.

Table 3 summarizes the results of this exercise.

The top five industries in terms of new water use priority are: Business Services, Local Transportation, Wholesale Trade, Sawmills, and New Construction. The bottom five are all identified by zeros in the valuation coefficient.

Remember, these industries are ranked by their direct and indirect effects on the State of Minnesota's employment. Other criteria could be applied and

Table 3 ✦ Water Values for Minnesota Based on the Objective of Maximizing

Employment Industry Title	Employment Objective Value Coefficient	Rank of Industry by Value Coefficient	Employment Industry Title	Employment Objective Value Coefficient	Rank of Industry by Value Coefficient
Dairy and Poultry	1.05	60	Primary Copper Prd	2.98	34
Meat Animals	0.62	65	Other Prim. Metal Prd	1.40	54
Food and Feed Crops	0.62	64	Fabricated Metal Prd	1.46	51
Other Crops	1.83	47	Farm Machinery	2.87	35
Forestry, Fish Svs	5.43	18	Machine Shops	6.02	16
Other Agriculture Svs	0.90	62	Non-Electric Mach	3.90	24
Iron & Ferrous Mng	0.35	67	Computing Machines	6.34	15
Nonferrous Mining	0.32	68	Service & Office Mach	3.71	25
Coal & Peat Mining	0.00	72	Electrical Machinery	2.36	43
Oil & Gas Drilling	0.00	73	Motor Vehicles	2.78	38
Stone & Clay Mng	0.44	66	Other Trans Equip	2.82	37
Other Mining	0.00	71	Professl, Sci Equip	4.36	21
New Construction	8.78	5	Optical & Photo Equip	3.03	33
Maintenance Constn	3.17	30	Misc Equipment	4.25	22
Ordinance	4.55	19	Railroad Trans	7.39	10
Meat Production	0.89	63	Local Transport	11.81	11
Dairy Production	1.22	56	Truck Transport	8.04	8
Canned & Fruit Prd	1.72	49	Air Transportation	3.47	27
Grain Milling	1.33	55	Other Transportation	5.50	17
Bakery Products	3.09	31	Communications	6.82	13
Beverages	1.15	59	Electric Companies	0.08	70
Misc Food Prd	1.16	57	Gas Utilities	1.95	46
Textile Mills	2.64	40	Water & Sanitary Svs	1.46	52
Knitting & Woolens	7.27	12	Wholesale Trade	8.92	3
Logging	8.36	6	Retail Trade	7.29	11
Sawmills	8.87	4	Finance & Insurance	4.41	20
Other Wood Products	3.34	28	Real Estate	2.39	42
Furniture	3.05	32	Hotels, Personal Svs	2.84	36
Pulp and Paper	1.75	48	Business Services	20.06	1
Paperboard	2.75	39	Eating & Drinking Est	7.72	9
Printing & Publishing	3.63	26	Automotive Services	6.75	14
Chemical & Allied Prd	2.01	45	Motion Picture	4.16	23
Petroleum Refining	0.96	61	Health Services	2.63	41
Rubber Products	1.52	50	Education	8.22	7
Leather Products	2.07	44	All Government Svs	3.28	29
Stone, Clay & Glass Prd	1.16	58	Scrap, 2ndhand Goods	0.0	74
Primary Ferrous Prd	0.26	69	Government Adm	0.0	75
Iron & Steel Products	1.45	53			

a similar analysis conducted. For example, one might want to look at the importance of these various industries from the supply side point of view; i.e., which industries are crucial in terms of supplying intermediate products so that the remaining industries could remain viable. The objective chosen will strongly influence the results.

Applying the Concept of the Multiplier to a Regional Economy

Richard Lichty
University of Minnesota–Duluth

What is this "multiplier" business all about anyway? How can multipliers be applied in a regional setting? What difference does it make talking about a multiplier for the United States as a whole or a multiplier for a smaller, regional economy? To what use are multipliers put at the national or the regional level?

A multiplier simply traces through rounds of activity that result from an initial outside (exogenous) shock to the economy. Multipliers can apply to various kinds of activities, such as: income, employment, output, or value added. The original discussion of multipliers by John Maynard Keynes dealt with income multipliers.

An income multiplier traces through rounds of income generation (or loss) due to an influx of new income (an outflow of existing income) into (out of) an identified region. For example, what if a new factory were to open in a city. That new factory would hire workers and pay them an income. In addition, that new factory may pay local landowners rent, local capital owners interest, and if the factory had local owners, local profits would even be generated. In short, the new factory means direct new income from several sources (wages, interest, rents, and profits).

But this is not the end of the story. Let's say that $1,000 of new income is brought into the region because of the new plant (it's a small plant). This means $1,000 of income to local people. What do people do with income? They spend it, or at least a part of it.

Let's say someone saves an average of $.20 out of every extra dollar made. Then the marginal propensity to save (MPC) is equal to .2. Let's say that everyone working at the plant has the same propensity to save. Then an extra $1,000 translates into $800 in new spending, ignoring the taxes and the possibility that some of this spending might leave the region for imported goods and services.

The economy now has $1,800; $1,000 in the direct increase in local income from the new plant and $800 as a second round of spending. But that is still not the end of the story.

The $800 that was spent in the second round was for other local goods and services. Someone had to apply labor, land, capital and enterprise towards the production of these other goods and services. In return, these "second round" providers expect what? Income. And if their propensities to save are the same .2 discussed earlier, they will spend .8 × $800, or $640 in the "third round."

People will spend .8 × $640 in the fourth round, or $512. People will spend .8 × $512 in the fifth round, or $409.60. On this process goes until the effect from the new plant has played itself out.

What is the total amount of new income in the region from the introduction of this new plant? It could be determined by adding $1,000 + $800 + $640 + $409.60 + ... Such an exercise would not be particularly fun. Fortunately, there is a short cut procedure for calculating multipliers.

Something puts a limit on the number of rounds of spending that can take place. If there wasn't, a $1,000 fusion into the economy would lead to an infinite number of rounds of new spending. It would only take a small exogenous change to lead to an unlimited increase in total regional income.

In the example above, the thing that reduces each round from the last is savings. Savings represents the withholding of spending. Withholding spending also withholds new income. So, if some percentage of each extra dollar earned is withheld, each round of new spending will be lower than the last.

What other withholdings might there be? Two come to mind: taxes and imports. Taxes (especially taxes directly applied to income or to spending) have the same effect as savings. Money sent to government is money withheld from local consumption.

Imports also have the same effect as savings. Money spent on goods and services produced elsewhere is money withheld from local consumption (and income).

Now one might protest that taxes wind up as government spending and that imports are at least partially offset by exports. And that is right. But here the discussion is what affects the size of the multiplier. Where new spending originates will be discussed later.

Savings, taxes, and imports are referred to as "leakages" from the income stream. They are leaks in that they reduce the size of each round of spending. The multiplier effect can be summarized by using these leakages.

Let's go back to pretending that savings is the only leakage and is equal to .2 of each new dollar earned. The effect from a new plant entering the region directly generating $1,000 worth of new income could be summarized by taking $1/.2 \times \$1,000 = 5 \times \$1,000 = \$5,000$. Add $1,000 + $800 + $640 + . . . and the result is $5,000.

The multiplier is equal to 1/leakages; in this case, 1/.2. If the multiplier times any new outside (exogenous) change in spending is taken, the result is the total direct and indirect effect on the economy.

There is really no difference in concept between regional and national multipliers. The description immediately above can fit both economic levels quite nicely. There are differences in emphasis, however.

Keynes developed his multiplier theory for national economies. He was trying to explain how an economy might stabilize at less than full employment, a notion that was not accepted prior to Keynes's work. (Keynes wrote during the Great Depression of the 1930s.)

Keynes emphasized savings, taxes, and government spending in his work. While he or she talked about international trade, this was clearly not his emphasis. His most general contention was that government should step in with either increases in spending or decreases in taxes whenever the national economy was experiencing unacceptable levels of unemployment. New government spending or decreased levels of taxes would provide the exogenous spending power against which the multiplier could work. Increasing incomes would result in increasing employment levels as the economy spends its way out of a recession (depression).

Regional analysts look more at trade as the development source because regional economies are much more dependent on trade than national economies.

Think about this for a second. If someone eats in a local restaurant and is presented with a bill for $40, how much of that $40 is really a local impact? Was the food grown in the community? Probably not. Were the materials that were used in constructing the restaurant produced in the region? Probably not. The plates? The silverware? The list could go on and on. Most of that $40 is imported into the region.

What is local in the above example? The services of the waitstaff, the cooks, the bartenders, perhaps the owner, and management. These are all local, the rest is imported. Perhaps $30 of the $40 is not local at all.

This also applies to exports. Exports have a positive impact on both national and on regional economies. However, many regional practitioners think that exports represent not only an important factor in explaining regional economic development, but they might represent the most important factor.

Whereas Keynesian theory emphasizes government spending and taxation policy variables for economic growth, the regional multipliers often emphasize exports. For one thing, if regional policy attempts to grow the economy through increases in local government spending, the leakage from imports will find much (perhaps most) of that new spending impacting the rest of the world and not the local economy.

The export base multiplier is found by dividing total regional activity by regional export activity, or: $e = T/X$, where e represents the export base multiplier, T represents total economic activity in the region, and X represents that portion of total local activity that is devoted to producing goods and services for export.

What is meant by "activity" in this regard? The same thing meant by the national (Keynesian) multiplier. Economic activity can be measured in terms of income, employment, value added, output, or many other possibilities. The Keynesian multiplier emphasized income. Job creation seems to be a consistent focal point for local economic policies.

The multiplier works something like this: Suppose there are 1,000 total jobs in the region and 250 of them are found to be related to export activity. The multiplier is then $1,000/250 = 4$. Now this multiplier can be related to a new facility moving into the region. Let's say the new facility is expected to employ 50 individuals producing commodities for export. Simply take the multiplier of 4 times the 50 new exporting individuals to obtain a total impact estimate of 200 new employees (including the original 50 employees).

There are many ways to estimate the percentage of total employment devoted to export activity. The most direct (and the most expensive) is to survey local businesses. There are a number of less direct estimation possibilities as well, the easiest being the so-called location quotient method. This method is a procedure partially employed to estimate the impact of a new aircraft manufacturing facility to be built in Duluth, Minnesota, in 1994.

As mentioned before, the location quotient is a procedure for estimating the denominator value of the export base multiplier. It makes some assumptions that are a bit scary, but it is also a cheap and quick procedure to use.

The location quotient simply divides the percentage of economic activity in an identified regional industry by the percentage of economic activity for that same industry for the nation as a whole. The formula is:

$$\frac{R_i/R}{N_i/N}$$

where: R_i is the level of economic activity in industry i located in the region being studied, R is total regional activity, N_i is the level of economic activity in industry i for the nation, and N is total national activity.

If the location quotient value is equal to one, the regional activity in that industry is the same as for the nation. One of the crucial assumptions of this approach is that the nation is generally self-sufficient in the production of all commodities. If the region has the same percentage of employment in an industry as does the nation, the conclusion is that the region is also self-sufficient in the production of that particular industrial commodity.

If the location quotient value is greater than one, the conclusion is that the region is producing more than it needs for local production. The excess is then applied to the export sector.

If the location quotient value is less than one, the region is not producing enough to meet its own needs. The deficit must be imported into the region.

Only the surplus activity is assigned to the export sector. Therefore, only the surplus activity is included in the denominator of the export base multiplier.

A combination of techniques were applied to analyzing the impact from a new aircraft manufacturing plant in Duluth, Minnesota. Table 1 on page 60 summarizes the industries used and the level of export activity associated with those industries. Table 1 forms the basis for the employment multiplier that will be applied to the plant's expected operations. All economic activity for this exercise is stated in terms of employment.

The total employment in the region is seen to be 148,948. The employment assigned to export activity is 46,648. The export base multiplier for the region is therefore: 148,948/46,648 = 3.19.

A private aircraft manufacturing industry announced that they were looking at Duluth, Minnesota, as a possible site for a new facility in the city. The initial direct increase in employment would be fifteen individuals involved in design. The eventual employment possibility for the plant is estimated to be 125 persons.

Table 1 ✦ Industrial Categories and Estimated Export Employment, Duluth, Minnesota

Industry Category	Total Employment	Export Employment	Industry Category	Total Employment	Export Employment
Ag, Forest, Fish	2,694	0	Motor Vehicle Equip,		
Mining	13,681	13,681	Svc Stations	3,248	1,062
Construction	9,299	3,068	Eating & Drinking	8,476	2,119
Food & Kindred	2,338	117	Other Retail Stores	8,228	1,748
Textile Mills/Fabric	554	232	Banking & Credit	2,307	346
Printing, Publishing			Finance, Insurance,		
& Allied Prd	2,150	456	& Real Estate	2,989	445
Chemical & Allied	339	0	Business Services	1,934	97
Furniture, Lumber,			Repair Services	1,826	91
& Wood Prd	2,760	2,760	Household Services	742	0
Primary Metals	1,516	500	Other Personal Svs	4,422	663
Fabricated Metal	1,260	419	Entertainment	1,177	176
Machinery Except			Hospital & Medical	13,876	4,717
Electrical	2,343	117	Education	14,571	1,005
Electrical Mach,			Non-Profit &		
Equip, & Sup	198	0	Religious Services	4,144	230
Other Durables			Professional Svs	1,784	0
& Nondurables	6,549	3,444	Government	8,158	408
RR & Railwy Equip	4,011	4,011	Totals	148,948	46,648
Truck & Warehouse	1,752	876			
Other Transport	2,446	1,344			
Communications	2,008	301			
Utilities &					
Sanitary Services	2,964	17			
Wholesale	4,703	0			
Gen Merch, Retail	3,288	1,885			
Food, Bakery,					
& Dairy Stores	4,213	313			

Source of Employment Totals: Census of Population, 1980. **Source of Export Employment:** Combination of input-output study for Northeast Minnesota, Location Quotient Analysis for Northeast Minnesota, and Limited Interviews With People Knowledgeable With Specific Northeast Minnesota Industries. **Region For Analysis:** Seven Counties in Northeast Minnesota Known as the Arrowhead Region.

Developers and planners (not to mention the local Chamber of Commerce) are always interested in estimating the total impact from such a new facility. Using the multiplier as the means to provide such an estimate and if this procedure were done correctly, the total impact would be estimated to be $125 \times 3.19 = 399$ new employees.

There are several warnings associated with conducting such an analysis. First, several assumptions were required in order to use the location quotients as a basis for estimating the region's export employment levels. It is quite probable that some of these assumptions lead to an underestimation of export employment. If how the multiplier is calculated is studied, an underestimation of export employment is found that will lead to an overestimation of the size of the multiplier. The value, 3.19, is not unbelievable as a regional employment multiplier, but it is on the high edge of believability.

Second, the multiplier is assumed to be constant, even after the new facility has been constructed and begins its operations. This particular facility might be small enough so that it does not significantly change the structure of the local economy. However, when new facilities enter the region, the balance between export and total employment might well change. A complete analysis might look into the direction of that possible change.

Finally, the multiplier is the same for all industries. A thorough study would attempt to look at the multiplier effects of industries, one at a time. Industries that purchase many of their required intermediate products locally would exert a larger multiplier effect on the economy than would industries that deal mostly with outside suppliers for their intermediate goods requirements. Industry specific multipliers would provide a more accurate reflection of the structure of the economy in this regard. The export base multiplier is an average for all industries and suffers somewhat because of its generality.

On the other hand, export base multipliers are quick and easy to calculate. If a ballpark estimate is all that is necessary for planning purposes, export base would be the easiest to apply. For the purposes here, the export base multiplier does a good job in demonstrating how the income multiplier developed by John M. Keynes has been modified and applied to regional economic development issues.

ECONOMICS AND THE ENVIRONMENT: THE RESERVE MINING CASE

Richard Lichty

University of Minnesota–Duluth

One of the classic environmental court cases in U.S. history, still cited in textbooks, involved the Federal Environmental Protection Agency (EPA) and Reserve Mining Company. The case revolved around an attempt on the part of the EPA and others to completely eliminate Reserve Mining's disposal of waste water and nonmagnetic rock into Lake Superior. One of the more interesting aspects of the case are alternatives proposed by Professor Jerrold Peterson, Professor of Economics at the University of Minnesota–Duluth.

Taconite is a low-grade iron ore. Special initial stage processing is necessary to make taconite usable at the smelter. This "beneficiating" process was first used in Minnesota by Reserve Mining Company whose operations were located in Silver Bay, Minnesota.

Reserve Mining mined its ore at Babbitt, Minnesota, and transported the ore forty-seven miles to the Silver Bay plant. The ore was transported by train in the form of rock. The rock had to be ground to a finer level before entering the plant.

Once in the plant, the rock was crushed further into yet finer particles. These fine particles were then combined with large amounts of water to form a slurry.

The next stage of the beneficiating process represents one of the most interesting stages. The slurry, containing waste rock and iron ore, ran over rotating magnetic drums. These magnetic drums picked up the iron ore and left the waste rock to be discarded.

The iron ore particles were then rolled into marble-sized pellets. These pellets contained seventy-five percent iron, but at this "green" stage, they were too soft to ship. So the final stage of taconite processing involved firing the green pellets at very high temperatures until they were hard enough for shipment.

What happened to the waste rock in the Reserve Mining operation? The waste rock remained in a slurry form and was literally poured out of the plant into Lake Superior. Five hundred million gallons of water and 60,000 tons of nonmagnetic rock were dumped into Lake Superior every day. This amounted to over 20,888,000 tons of waste dumped into Lake Superior every year. The EPA decided that the waste tailings were a detriment to Lake Superior's ecology. A lengthy court process followed during which the EPA also contended that the tailings represented a health threat to the people along Lake Superior due to the discovery of asbestos like fibers in the tailings.

Northeast Minnesota has long been the center for iron mining in the United States. The first iron ore was discovered in the state in the late 1850s and was commercially mined in the middle 1860s. Mining really got under way in the early 1890s as the Missabe Range was discovered and exploited at that time. Mining went through ups and downs for several decades, peaking during World War II and the expansion years to follow.

It was shortly after World War II that fears began to emerge regarding the extent of remaining iron ore reserves in the region. At the rate that natural iron ore was being mined at that time, the ore deposits were scheduled to be fully depleted for commercial purposes somewhere in the late 1950s. While rich deposits were being discovered elsewhere in the world, concern over the northeast Minnesota economy and the iron and steel plants in the lower Great Lakes prompted exploration into alternative types of iron ore. Attention soon turned on the possibility of using a lower grade of iron ore called taconite. Taconite was seen to be relatively plentiful in the northeast Minnesota region.

The technology for taconite was not particularly new. Taconite processing technology of one form or another was fairly well known by the early 1900s. Commercial plants were attempted between 1929 and 1950, but none turned out to be commercial successes. The natural ore was cheaper to smelt than the lower grade taconite.

However, with the depletion of the natural ore in northeast Minnesota, attention turned to the taconite possibility once again. Planning and pilot plant developments occurred near Babbitt, Minnesota, between 1944 and 1951, leading to plans to develop the first full-scale taconite plant in northeast Minnesota in the town of Silver Bay. The taconite plant secured all necessary permits for operation, began construction in 1951, and began turning out a commercial product in 1955.

The natural ore had essentially run out by 1960. Much concern remained over the commercial viability of taconite as a sole ore in the smelting process. Taconite was more expensive to mine and develop than natural ore. These increased costs, plus uncertainty as to its viability in the smelting process, led ARMCO to experiment with using taconite in a modified smelter on a pilot basis. ARMCO reported the experiment to be a success, which led to a general boom in taconite plant investment in northeast Minnesota.

The plant in Silver Bay was a wholly-owned subsidiary of ARMCO and Republic Steel and was named Reserve Mining Company. Reserve Mining used ore out of a pit near Babbitt, Minnesota, processed the ore, and dumped the waste tailings into Lake Superior under a permit granted by the Minnesota Pollution Control Agency.

The dumping of taconite tailings into Lake Superior was obvious and quite visible to the casual observer. The plant did not exactly fit in with the natural surroundings and brown stains surrounded the otherwise pristine blue waters of Lake Superior around Silver Bay. Issues were raised pertaining to this dumping that eventually led to a 1974 court ruling by Federal Judge Miles Lord to close the plant. Judge Lord's order was overruled by the District Court of Appeals, which led to several years of court wrangling by Reserve Mining against a number of groups and agencies over whether the dumping of tailings would have to be stopped.

Reserve Mining leaned on the permits they obtained to use Lake Superior as a dump site, offered to establish a process whereby the tailings would be funneled to a deep hole in Lake Superior (which would mitigate against some of the sight problems with the dumping), and stated that they would go out of business with the loss of attending jobs if they had to dump on land. The opponents of Reserve argued that the permits did not allow the amount of dumping in which Reserve was currently engaged and, during the course of the trial, contended that the tailings contained asbestos-like fibers, a known carcinogen.

The final solution was for Reserve to develop on-land dumping ponds. In other words, after years of wrangling, Reserve did decide to stop their dumping into Lake Superior. Reserve Mining declared bankruptcy just a few years later and has been re-organized as a worker-owned facility.

Two issues were really at stake here. The first was that the court case allowed only two options: (1) Reserve Mining could continue to operate using Lake Superior as a dumping site for its wastes (although perhaps under an arrangement where the tailings would be funneled to a deep hole in the lake bottom), or (2) Reserve Mining could be forced to dump its tailings on land and perhaps be forced to close its operations if it could not or would not comply with the on-land order.

Professor Jerrold Peterson, outside of the litigation process, proposed a third alternative. Allow Reserve Mining to continue to operate but tax Reserve for the damage its operations did to the physical and social environment. If Reserve Mining could not profitably pay the tax, it would have to close down. If Reserve Mining could profitably pay the tax, it could continue to operate and the tax money could be used to help mitigate against the damage caused by Reserve's pollution.

When Reserve Mining engaged in the beneficiating process, two products emerged. The first was a relatively hard taconite pellet that represented the primary "good" produced by Reserve. The other was a waste product in the form of rock tailings that represented the primary "bad" produced by Reserve.

What is the criterion associated with how much of the good would be produced by Reserve? Reserve would continue to produce an additional unit of taconite pellets as long as the extra revenues it gained from the sale of that unit exceeded the extra costs from producing the unit. In other words, Reserve would continue to produce as long as marginal revenues exceeded marginal costs.

However, the technology associated with Reserve's operations was such that for every ton of taconite pellets produced, two tons of tailings were produced as a by-product. The number of tons of taconite tailings produced were determined by the number of tons of pellets produced, which were, in turn, determined by profit maximization considerations.

If a market is functioning perfectly, there would be no problem. The number of tons of pellets and tailings produced would be socially efficient in the following sense: The revenues received from production would represent society's willingness and ability to pay for iron ore (and ultimately for steel). Society's willingness and ability to pay represents the benefits side of Reserve's operations.

In order to produce these pellets, Reserve must use some of the productive resources available to the nation. The costs of those resources would reflect the opportunities society sacrificed by using these resources for taconite production as opposed to other possibilities.

By continuing to push production as long as marginal revenues exceed marginal costs, society is using the resources in such as way as to maximize the benefits over the opportunities foregone. If this were done for all commodities, net societal benefits (society benefits minus society costs) would be maximized.

Problems arise when not all benefits or not all costs are taken into account in the production decision. In the Reserve Mining instance, all of the costs are not taken into account. Why?

Reserve obviously takes into account the costs of the beneficiating process, including the costs of waste discharge. The costs Reserve does not take into account are those costs imposed on the rest of society because Lake Superior is no longer as clean as it was before and because the potential exists that lives could be lost due to the asbestos-like fibers in the water. The result of not taking these costs into account is that more taconite pellets (and more tailings) will be produced than are socially optimal.

Why more than optimal? Because costs are "too low" from society's point of view; a broader range of production will be possible where marginal revenues exceed marginal costs.

A cost of production that is outside of the considerations by a firm is called an external cost, or externality. In this case, the externality is the cost imposed on the rest of society by the operations of Reserve.

There are two possibilities. The first is that externalities exist from the first ton of tailings produced. This would be the case if any discharge of the asbestos like fibers into the lake posed a health risk or when even one ton of discharge has the effect of lowering the lake's viability in terms of alternative uses.

The other possibility assumes that ecosystems have some ability to clean themselves. Under this condition, if the lake has some ability to absorb waste without either noticeable damage to its ecosystem or to users of the lake's water resource, the externality does not exist until this absorption capacity is exceeded.

Figure 1 on page 68 represents an externality condition that assumes environmental damage from the first ton of tailings produced. The extent of environmental and human damage are assumed to increase as soon as the first ton is produced. This is depicted by the fact that the marginal social costs of production exceed the marginal private costs of production as soon as it moves from zero. The difference between the two represents the value of the marginal external cost society bears from Reserves operations.

Notice that the two cost curves diverge as production increases. The implicit assumption behind these diverging curves is that the damage to the lake's ecology and to the rest of society increases as the number of tailings dumped into the lake increases. There is a cumulative effect from increased tailings disposal into the lake, a reasonable assumption.

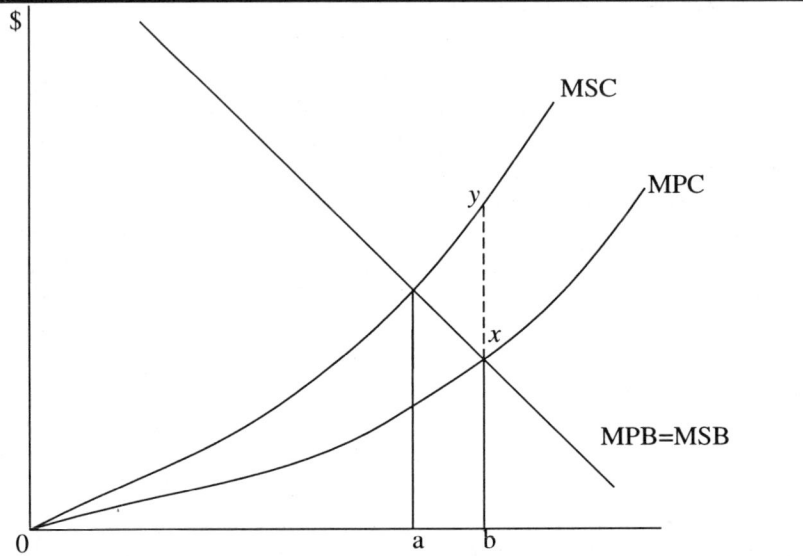

Figure 1 ✦ The external cost from Reserve's operations appears to society as a divergence between marginal social and marginal private costs. The marginal private cost to Reserve is the extra cost from dumping an extra ton of tailings. The marginal social cost is the additional costs to society from tailings disposal; costs which Reserve does not pay. The marginal social benefits and marginal private benefits curves are equal through the assumption that there are no "positive" externalities from Reserve's operations.

How many tailings would Reserve choose to dump into the lake under the conditions illustrated by Figure 1? Reserve only looks at its private costs and benefits in reaching such a decision. It would choose to produce where marginal private benefits (revenues) equal marginal private costs. The output is depicted in Figure 1 as the distance 0b.

How many tailings would society prefer to have Reserve dump into Lake Superior under the conditions illustrated by Figure 1? Society would choose to produce where marginal social benefits (based on a willingness and ability to pay) equal marginal social costs. The output is depicted in Figure 1 as the distance 0a.

Thus, Reserve is producing more taconite tailings (because it is producing more taconite pellets) than are socially optimal. Notice that, in this instance, society does not want Reserve to produce zero tailings. This last statement has interesting implications in light of the Reserve court case where zero discharge was being sought by EPA and its co-plaintiffs.

Figure 1 implicitly assumes that society wants taconite pellets (eventually leading to steel products). Society reflects this want by being willing and able to pay for these pellets a sum that exceeds costs in terms of other uses of the resource. In other words, Figure 1 shows a society that is willing to accept some social costs in return for iron ore production. Such would be true for most products produced.

The only way that society would opt for zero pollution associated with a desired good would be if the social costs were so high that they exceeded social benefits at every level of production. It could be that Polychlorinated Biphenyl (PCBs) fit this description. PCBs were found to be so deadly that even small production levels led to enormous social costs. In such a case, the only solution would be a zero discharge solution.

What are the policy implications from the analysis contained in Figure 1? There are really two market based possibilities in addition to the "zero discharge" solution. Both market based policy alternatives assume it is possible to measure the marginal damage from an additional unit (ton) of discharge into the lake.

The first market based policy would be for government to simply issue a rule that Reserve could dump no more than 0a units of tailings into the lake. Some kind of monitoring and policing mechanism would then need to be set up to keep track of Reserve's dumping levels.

The second would be to impose a tax on Reserve equal to the marginal damage done to the lake and to society. The marginal tax would be the difference between marginal private costs and marginal social costs at any level of production.

If Reserve were producing 0b units of waste prior to the policy, the initial tax would be equal to the distance xy with the tax falling every time production falls and the distance between MSC and MPC narrows. Under this condition, if Reserve were forced to pay to full costs of its operations (private and public), it would choose to produce less taconite tailings until production eventually reached 0a units. 0a units are what society deems to be the optimum.

The zero discharge solution takes us to two further possibilities. If zero discharge is achieved by finding an alternative dumping site, say on land as opposed to in the lake, and if Reserve can continue to profitably produce its product under such an arrangement, society has gained to the extent that there are no externalities associated with the land site. If there are externalities associated with the land option, then the analysis would have to begin all over again.

The second of these possibilities is that Reserve would not be able to maintain a profitable operation with a land site dumping arrangement. Reserve would close its operations under such conditions and no taconite would be produced out of the Silver Bay plant. Presumably, society wanted that taconite (or the steel that taconite eventually helped produce) enough to pay the firm a normal return once the society optimum is reached (referring to Figure 1 again). To cease these operations is to work against society's general interest in this regard, and material welfare is sacrificed.

The tax solution presumes that society will determine whether continued production is worthwhile through its willingness and ability to pay a price that is above costs, including social costs, of production. If not, Reserve would close as in the case where the company could not afford to pay for on-land disposal. But in the tax case, the closing is efficient from society's point of view. It closes in this case because society does not think the costs of production and dumping to be worth the benefits from the use of the taconite product.

Now we have all the necessary background for understanding Professor Peterson's analysis of the Reserve Mining controversy. He was attempting to determine an appropriate marginal tax equal to the marginal social damage associated with Reserve's dumping into Lake Superior.

There are two kinds of social cost discussed in Professor Peterson's work. The first he or she called "implicit costs." These are the costs associated with Reserve Mining using Lake Superior at no cost. If Reserve were to have gone on land with its tailings disposal, there would be the costs of land rent, land preparation, and perhaps, land reclamation. Reserve avoided these costs by using Lake Superior for free. Professor Peterson contended that the government should have the right to claim payments for the use of this otherwise public resource.

Another implicit cost is associated with the loss of the use of the land for other purposes. For example, certain recreational uses of the land become unfeasible due to a phenomenon associated with the tailings discharge. The so-called "green water" phenomenon found a rather unattractive greenish brown hue expanding along the north shore of the lake. This hue was directly attributed to the tailings discharge. It reduced the value of recreational property wherever it appeared.

The other category of social costs are called "explicit costs." Explicit costs are the direct costs of protecting society from the harms of the tailings discharge. Water treatment and filtration plants for communities using the water were found to be one category of explicit cost. The loss of human life was another.

One might be tempted to say at this point, "Wait a minute. If the loss of human life occurs because of the tailings discharge, there can be no benefit-cost analysis. We can't put a value on human life—the value is infinite."

Economists answer that the economic value of life is not infinite. People don't behave as if it were. For example, every time someone gets in a car and drives to school or work, he or she takes a risk of sustaining an injury so severe that it leads to a loss of life.

Why would anyone risk such a valuable commodity as his or her own life. Because he or she deems that the benefits from work or schooling exceed the probability of being killed in route. Sure the probability of disaster is small. But it is there. And that small probability, when compared to the benefits received, persuades people to go to work or school tomorrow just as it persuaded them to go to work or school today. This meant that Professor Peterson had to include an estimate for the value of life in his explicit cost calculations.

Table 1 presents Professor Peterson's findings. Most of the categories are fairly straightforward. The cost of lake eutrophication includes the costs associated with the loss of recreational value due to the tailings discharge. It also includes the loss of such things as aquatic life as a result of the waste discharge.

The health hazard issue was mentioned previously. Professor Peterson dealt with the economic value of a human life by estimating the loss of earnings to the economy due to early deaths associated with asbestos fibers in the water. In other words, Professor Peterson argued that society's loss of potential worker productivity due to an untimely death constituted the real economic cost (and human life value lost) from Reserve's operations.

The residual cost contains the interest rate associated with the use of the resource over time. Professor Peterson used the existing rate of 6.93 percent

TABLE 1 ✦ Professor Peterson's Estimates of Social Costs

Type of Costs	Social Cost From Reserve's Operations
Use of Lake Bottom	*$4,756,000*
Lake Eutrophication	*3,837,000*
Water Filtration	*484,000*
Health Hazard	*1,064,000*
Residual	*$11,506,000*

attached to U.S. long-term bonds. The remaining categories of cost are self-explanatory.

If Professor Peterson's social cost estimates are correct and given that Reserve Mining's discharge at the time of Peterson's work was 20,888,000 tons of tailings per annum, calculating the per ton effluent charge is fairly straightforward. Divide the $11,888,000 by the annual discharge to arrive at a charge of $0.55 per ton.

What are the probable effects from such a charge? First of all, Reserve could have avoided the charge by switching the disposal to land. Zero discharge into Lake Superior means a zero pollution charge.

Second, Reserve could have avoided a portion of the charge by reducing (but not eliminating) its output. Review Figure 1 and the discussion on Figure 1 for an analysis of this possibility.

Third, the government would receive the $11,888,000 annually. This money could be used to: (1) build sophisticated and up-to-date water filtration systems for the communities along the lake's shore, (2) provide for health screening in an attempt to detect early signs of disease (cancer primarily) brought on by Reserve's tailings operations, and (3) where necessary, compensate resort owners, homeowners, and other identified recreational users for the loss of recreational values associated with the green water phenomenon. Any money left over could be used by government for other purposes since it would be associated with the rent of the lake, rent that was then being avoided by Reserve by using the lake for free.

Agreement with Professor Peterson's every calculation really does not matter. It should be clear that there is a great deal of "guestimation" associated with studies of this type.

However, taxing effluents is the economist's recommendation for dealing with pollution of this type. Why? Because it relies mostly on individual judgements and behavior for solving the problem, which is consistent with the principles of free enterprise. Judgements and behavior in a market system are based on incentives. The tax puts such an incentive system in place and then allows market forces to play themselves out.

There may be debate on the accuracy of the figures, but there are also debates over government attepts to directly regulate effluent discharge. One advantage of Peterson's approach is that the debate focuses on the actual damage done and not of the politics of jobs versus the environment. If businesses go out of business because they cannot afford the tax, the market says those jobs should have been lost anyway. It is the way the market system works.